T0318440

"This timely and accessible volume suggests an innovative approach to managing the changing context of aging and work, and is, importantly, relevant to all ages of workers. Moving beyond generational stereotypes and outdated age-based policies, the authors suggest an evidence-based strategy that has led to successful outcomes for employees, their families, and the organizations they inhabit."

Jacquelyn B. James, Co-Director of the Sloan Research Network on Aging and Work, Boston College, USA

"Grounded in scientific research but also comprehensive and entertaining, this book is a very useful guide for managers, HR professionals, and politicians to address the demographic changes in work organizations. In addition to concrete tools and concepts, the authors also consider aging in light of global changes, such as digitization of work or the COVID-19 pandemic. Highly needed, and fun to read!"

Guido Hertel, Dean of the University Department of Psychology and Sports Science, University of Münster, Germany

Ageless Talent

Ageless Talent: Enhancing the Performance and Well-Being of Your Age-Diverse Workforce provides organizational leaders, managers, and supervisors with clear, evidence-based tactics by which to develop and manage an aging and age-diverse talent pool. This volume provides an easy-to-implement set of tools for addressing the difficult problems related to employee performance and well-being amid ongoing technological and social change.

Ageless Talent introduces a straightforward framework (PIERA) that translates scientific advances into actionable steps and strategies. Using this framework, this book provides practical illustrations to help readers design their own small-scale interventions to achieve desirable goals under diverse organizational constraints. Furthermore, the book addresses modern management challenges arising across the globe, and offers suggestions for leaders interested in short-term and long-term change. These suggestions, grounded in time-tested and leading-edge research evidence, include specific step-by-step guidelines, customizable to different types of organizations and industries.

With economic, cultural, technological, and demographic shifts making the changing nature of work a pressing concern for organizations around the globe, *Ageless Talent* is an essential text for practitioners – HR professionals, organizational leaders, and managers – as well as management education programs and professional training and leadership programs. It will also appeal to instructors and students in the field of industrial/organizational psychology.

Lisa M. Finkelstein is Professor of Industrial / Organizational Psychology at Northern Illinois University. She is Fellow of the Society for Industrial and Organizational Psychology and Associate Investigator at the ARC Centre of Excellence in Population Ageing Research.

Donald M. Truxillo is Professor at the Kemmy Business School, University of Limerick, Ireland and Professor Emeritus at the Industrial / Organizational Psychology Program at Portland State University. He is Fellow of the Society for Industrial and Organizational Psychology, the American Psychological Association, and the Association for Psychological Science.

Franco Fraccaroli is Professor of Organizational Psychology at Trento University, Italy. He is Fellow of the Society for Industrial and Organizational Psychology and the International Association of Applied Psychology. He served as President of the European Association of Work and Organizational Psychology.

Ruth Kanfer is Professor of Psychology and Director of the Work Science Center at Georgia Institute of Technology. She is Fellow of the Society for Industrial and Organizational Psychology, the Association for Psychological Science, the American Psychological Association, and the Academy of Management.

Ageless Talent

Enhancing the Performance
and Well-Being of Your Age-Diverse
Workforce

**LISA M. FINKELSTEIN, DONALD M. TRUXILLO,
FRANCO FRACCAROLI, AND RUTH KANFER**

Routledge
Taylor & Francis Group

NEW YORK AND LONDON

First published 2021
by Routledge
605 Third Avenue, New York, NY 10158

and by Routledge
2 Park Square, Milton Park, Abingdon, Oxon, OX14 4RN

Routledge is an imprint of the Taylor & Francis Group, an informa business

Library of Congress Cataloging-in-Publication Data
A catalog record has been requested for this book

ISBN: 978-0-367-34569-3 (hbk)
ISBN: 978-0-367-34568-6 (pbk)
ISBN: 978-0-429-32660-8 (ebk)

Typeset in Dante and Avenir
by KnowledgeWorks Global Ltd.

For Kurt, who as a worker, human, and life partner is a true model for getting better with age.

-LMF

For Chip

-DMT

For Alba, a mature but young worker.

-FF

For Phillip, Sarah, and the future of work dignity.

-RK

Contents

x Contents

Preface

In 2015, a book edited by the four of us called *Facing the Challenges of a Multi-Age Workforce: A Use-Inspired Approach* hit the shelves. This book was part of the Society for Industrial and Organizational Psychology's (SIOP) Frontiers Book Series, designed to set a research agenda to address the urgent needs of an aging workforce. Shortly after it was released, two of us were invited to represent this book and speak at a US Congressional Briefing on Capitol Hill on evidence-based solutions to the challenges of workforce aging sponsored by SIOP. At that event, we distributed copies of our book to those who wanted them. At the end of that event, we found ourselves wondering if anyone in that audience would actually read our book.

Don't get us wrong – we are very proud of that book. It contains many gems written by leading scholars, suggesting the research that is needed to tackle urgent, real-world problems. But the book's audience was primarily academic researchers and scholars. A seed was planted: we needed to write a practice-focused book that was based in science but would help managers, leaders, and policy-makers with practical suggestions to apply right now.

The book in your hand (or on your tablet) is that book we envisioned. It was created to provide organizational leaders at all levels with clear, evidence-based tactics by which to develop and manage an aging and age-diverse talent pool. We built it on the science of the psychology of work. We then translate that science into an easy-to-implement set of tools for facing the sometimes difficult problems related to employee well-being, motivation, interpersonal relationships, and performance that have arisen in the midst of ongoing technological and global social change.

And although much was already changing in the world of work and in the demographics of the workforce, there was no way we would have predicted that we would be finishing this book in the midst of a global pandemic that would turn the world of work – and pretty much all of the world – on its head. Indeed, the writing of this book was impacted by the pandemic. The authors lost their opportunities to meet and discuss it face-to-face, fears of the pandemic affected our lives and disturbed the tranquility necessary to devote ourselves to writing, and in fact some pages were written by an author in recovery from the virus.

We are not fortune tellers, or even futurists. We recognize that there is no way to foresee exactly how work, the workplace, and workers will change as a result of this unique and challenging period in history. There are, however, a growing number of indicators showing that older employees are in an increasingly difficult position. Remote work has, for many older workers, required new learning of platforms like Zoom. At the same time, organizations appear less likely to rehire older workers. And many older employees have been forced to choose between their own safety and continuing to work. For some older employees, these forces have resulted in unplanned early retirement and search for alternative employment.

At the same time, the pandemic has affected younger workers more severely in different ways. For example, a report from the Organisation for Economic Co-operation and Development (OECD)[1] conveys that younger people, especially women, may be most affected economically due to their higher level of employment in precarious or fixed-term jobs as well as in industries, such as hospitality, most affected by this crisis.

These issues inspired us to go back through our chapters and acknowledge some specific examples of the ways COVID-19 has begun to impact work. Additionally, we believe our PIERA method – which we will introduce in Chapter 2 – can be used to address specific acute and urgent workplace challenges as well as the more chronic and ongoing challenges that leaders face as work and workers evolve.

We want to thank our editor, Christina Chronister, for her gracious assistance at all phases of this project, and Danielle Dyal, who helped us bring it all together at the end. We also want to thank the organizations and individuals who allowed us to provide the case studies throughout this book.

And thank you for picking up our book. We think that means that you see the need for leaders to address these issues around age and work. We think that this book will give you the evidence-based tools you need to do so. We also hope you choose to roll up your sleeves and try out some ideas.

Note

1. OECD. (2020). *Youth and COVID-19: Response, recovery and resilience.* Available at: https://www.oecd.org/coronavirus/policy-responses/youth-and-covid-19-response-recovery-and-resilience-c40e61c6/

Work Is Evolving, and So Are Workers

1

Let's Prepare for That

Imagine this scenario. You are leaving the office in the early evening to head home after a busy day. You glance into the glass-walled conference room and see a team of employees from another group gathering around as if they are setting up a meeting. You notice the wide-screen TV on the wall has a team from Singapore joining in remotely – that must explain the odd hour to begin a meeting! The group at the table looks to range from their early 20s to maybe even their 70s, and they seem to run the gamut of styles, cultures, and genders. Some appear to look a bit impatient to be starting a meeting so late in the day; they likely had to do a work-life juggling act to make this work. As a young woman, the leader of the team, seems to be calling the meeting to order, each person has a smartphone out on the table or is not-so-stealthily using them in their laps. There are some pizza boxes out on the table – looks like they might be there a while.

Most of our own workplaces contain at least some elements from this scene. Our work-nonwork lines have blurred. Technology infuses most of what we do and seems to change as soon as we become used to it. Our team members may be located all over the world, and even those across the table from us may not only look different from us on multiple levels but also see the world, and our work challenges, through a very different life-experience lens.

These are important observations about the world of work, but they aren't exactly earth-shattering news to most of us. People have been talking and writing about this stuff for a long time. So what's different about our approach in this book?

We believe there are a lot of complex and dynamic changes happening to work on a worldwide scale. Many of these demographic, technological, cultural, and even economic shifts work in sync to affect workers in new ways[1] – and how any particular worker responds to this tide of change depends largely on their life stage and the particular, unique experiences that brought them to where they are today. And where they are today is not where they will be next year or maybe even next quarter. Workers are ever evolving – just like work.

Generational Rough Cuts: Inadequate and Misleading

We're guessing that when you hear about "today's workers", what you are typically hearing about is the influx of Millennials, or perhaps even the newer workers, often called Gen Z. These younger generations are sometimes discussed as if they have landed on earth from another planet and have an entirely different set of needs, motivations, and working styles. If your organization is going to keep up, they say, you need to get in the heads of these Millennial workers. Furthermore, "these workers" are discussed as if they were all the same person and that there was no variability among them. People born after 1980 are talked about with such sweeping generalizations as if they don't differ in terms of background, experience, personality, and skills.

This is definitely *not* the approach that we take in this book. This generational approach to understanding changing work and workers assumes arbitrary cut points to determine generational groups. It tends to make vast oversimplifications about all members of these groups, lumping all people born within this time period together. What's more, it tends to feed into an "us-versus-them" mentality and foster stereotyping. This type of approach begets a sort of "Millennials are from Mars, Gen Xers are from Jupiter" approach that is unlikely to be very helpful to anyone, including those managing them.[2]

Perhaps it would be nice to be able to rely on what we learn in the media about Millennials' strengths, weaknesses, and challenges – we would have a preview of what all our new employees are like, and we wouldn't have to worry about it until the next arbitrary generation cutoff date. But, alas, it isn't quite that simple. You wouldn't make assumptions (we hope!) about the needs, preferences, values, and skills of all women, all men, or all people from a certain ethnic group. Why do it for the hundreds of millions of people worldwide that are tagged with these generational labels (or for any other generation, for that matter)? Although there are certainly influences that impact people who are the same age at the same historical time period on average differently than those of a different age at that time period, making assumptions about your new direct report based *solely* on their generational group can lead to a host of misunderstandings and even missed opportunities.[3,4] Sometimes it's hard to convince people of this because they think they "see with their own two eyes" the differences among their team members belonging to different generations.

This book will help show that there is a lot more going on, however, than simply a person's generational status. It is rare to see a book for managers that addresses the variety of ways workers can change, mature, and evolve over the course of their work lives and depending on their life circumstances. In this book, we borrow from the latest research in work and organizational psychology, gerontology, HRM sciences, and sociology to present some practical ways to understand your evolving workers – regardless of their age. It will provide you with some tools to better manage all your employees – from different age groups, and over time as they change and develop.

The Dynamic and Shifting Workscape

It is impossible to talk about how workers change over the lifespan without considering the changing nature of workplaces, workspaces, and job demands. These things affect everyone regardless of age or life stage, or course, but they may not affect us all in the same way.

What's more, all these changes may interact in many ways. For example, we will talk about some cultural issues – work practices aren't the same everywhere, and aging workers are seen and treated differently by different cultures (see our Special Focus Box 1.1 for more on this). This was always the case, but now that technology has us more readily interacting in teams across cultures, the impact of these differences can affect us all. Let's take a closer look at what's happening in today's workscape, and why it matters for the aging workforce.

For instance, consider demographic shifts around the world. The decline in birthrate and increase in life expectancy are catching up with society. To illustrate, right now in the European Union, there are four working people for every retired person.[5] If the retirement norms and immigration trends do not change, how many will that be in 2060? Only

Special Focus Box 1.1: An International Perspective

Your authors include two Americans living in the United States, an expat American living in Ireland, and a native Italian living in his homeland. We recognize that there are different laws and policies in different countries regarding things like age discrimination and retirement age, and these can shape the culture around age and work in that country. Here we provide just a few examples for you and some resources for you to find out information about how these laws may impact your strategies for managing age at work. These examples come from a fuller and more detailed list at agediscrimination.info/international.

Country	Laws
The USA	The Age Discrimination in Employment Act (ADEA) of 1967 makes it unlawful for an employer to discriminate (in terms of hiring, compensation, firing, terms and conditions of employment, etc.) against workers over 40 years of age.
Canada	Canada's Charter of Rights and Freedom (1982; Section 15-1) bans age discrimination along with other forms of discrimination. The different provinces have slight variations on who is covered; Alberta, Ontario, and Saskatchewan ban it toward those over age 9, British Columbia over age 18, while others do not specify.
Italy	Article 15 of the Workers' Statute (1970) prohibits age discrimination (no age specified) in hiring dismissal, discipline, or other damages. The EU Framework Directive no. 78/2000 (2002) further protects from indirect forms of discrimination, such as harassment.
Ireland	The Employment Equality Acts (EEA) of 1998 to 2015 prohibit discrimination in employment in terms of access, conditions of employment, training opportunities, promotion, etc. for employees of any age above the maximum age that they must attend school (currently 16).
New Zealand	The New Zealand Bill of Rights Act (1990) includes protection from age discrimination. Complaints can be filed under the Human Rights Commission or Employee Relations Authority; remedies are meant to be compensatory and not punitive or criminal.
Singapore	The Retirement and Re-employment Act (Chp 274A) or Singapore protects employees from dismissal based on age prior to mandatory retirement age of 62 or what is specified contractually (whatever is higher).

| Israel | Age discrimination is prohibited under the Employment Equal Opportunities Law. The law was enacted in 1988 but didn't cover age until 1995. There is no specified age to make a claim. |
| Kenya | The Constitution of Kenya (2010) prohibits discrimination from the State on the basis of age, among other things. The Employment Act of 2007 (5-2 and 5-3) prohibits employment discrimination. It does not mention age expressly, but has been used in conjunction with the Constitution to make age discrimination claims. |

Additional Resources on Employment Law

Murphy, K. R. (2018). The legal context of the management of human resources. *Annual Review of Organizational Psychology and Organizational Behavior, 5*, 157–182.

Myors, B., et al. (2008). International perspectives on the legal environment for selection. *Industrial and Organizational Psychology, 1*, 206–246.

Ryan, A. M., & Tippins, N. (2009). *Designing and implementing global selection systems.* Malden, MA: Wiley-Blackwell.

two working people for every retired person! The potential economic ramifications of these trends are staggering. Although the projected change in the United States is not so dramatic, the pattern is similar. For countries to be able to support their older population, it will be imperative for people to work longer. But for people to do that, we must do what we can do to ensure good health and sustained motivation and productivity. Creative and flexible policies are needed.

There are other economic, technological, and cultural changes and challenges that accompany this demographic shift as well. For example, changes to the public welfare systems in many countries will necessitate longer careers, and this may result in fewer opportunities for younger workers to find stable employment with growth potential.

Age will continue to have a significant impact on key jobs. Certain fields are experiencing growth and others contraction. Skill sets among workers from different age groups do not match these changing dynamics. For instance, the medical field is growing and in need of skilled and highly educated workers to handle the huge increases in the older population and its associated health issues.[6] It likely comes as no surprise that the tech industry is growing rapidly as well. The flipside, however, is that certain industries are dying out. Older workers in fields that are no longer thriving find themselves laid off and face difficulties getting re-employed. If not faced with unemployment, many will be overqualified for the work they are able to secure (and perhaps underpaid). Increasingly, they will be working for and with people many years their junior. Interestingly, it may not be only because technological advancements make workers in some industries passé; some type of work may be less in demand because of the technological changes in our nonwork life. When's the last time you paid a visit to your local watch repair or camera repair store?[7]

Within almost all jobs, even the more traditional ones, technological changes have implications for training needs. Managers and workers must accept lifelong learning at the "new normal" to stay productive and successful. And not only is technology often the trigger for training, it may also be present in the *mode* of training as well. Computer-based training can be cost-effective and practical, but may instigate fear and hesitation in those not as familiar with new technology.[8] Many older people are keenly adept at using new technology, but on average the skill level is likely to be higher among younger folks who have been using technology since they were in diapers.

Technology has also afforded us the "luxury" of being able to work from remote locations in many types of jobs; that luxury, however, can also be a curse when it is accompanied by the expectation that if someone *can* work everywhere, they *should* always be working![9] This type of telepressure may impact workers differently at different stages of their life course, depending on their nonwork demands and preferences, but for many it can lead to technostress.

On a similar note, technological changes allow us to now more easily collaborate with people all over the world. This has led to an increase in virtual teams. These types of teams have communication obstacles regardless of the demographic composition of the team, but may have an added challenge if team members are diverse in age and hail from cultures that have different norms regarding interage communication and expectations about how long people can and should remain employed.[10]

These tech changes in the mode of communication for work tasks also affect the social fabric of organizational life, as people have fewer opportunities for or inclinations toward water cooler chatter and are increasingly interacting via social media. Increased diversity not only in age but also in other cultural dimensions can lead on the one hand to richer communication and social experiences, but on the other to concern and sensitivity to language and manner.

As readers of this book you come from different industries and are more or less affected by these changes, but we can't imagine any reader not impacted in some way by these workplace challenges. Merely keeping your head above water to weather today's changes is not an option; being proactive in preparing for what lies ahead is necessary. As economist Richard Baldwin says, "the future doesn't take appointments".[11]

Understanding Workers as Continuously Developing Beings

It is surprisingly easy to think about employees as interchangeable. Yet we know that employees differ in many ways, in terms of personality, skills, and other differences that affect productivity. But one way that has often been overlooked is how people differ as a function of their life experiences and changes in physical and cognitive abilities over the life course. Gerontologists, developmental psychologists, work and organizational psychologists, human factors specialists, and HR and management professionals are conducting important research on how "people changes" over the lifespan affect workability and job attitudes. Although it has long been believed that workers necessarily deteriorate with age, it turns out that it is not so simple. The research does indeed show that, on average, there are physical declines that eventually come with aging, as well as some cognitive declines that affect how well we remember and process new information.[12] The good news, however, is that age-related physical declines are being pushed back to later in life, and that there may be some advances that come with age. For those reasons, for a growing number of people, paid employment may extend well beyond traditional retirement ages.

Although the notion of loss in physical and mental competencies during later adulthood is deeply embedded in most cultures, there is also research to show some important advantages of aging. For example, people tend to acquire knowledge through experiences as they age. They also are better able to regulate their emotions, optimize resources, and hone their social skills.[13] A real-world demonstration of this cocktail of advantages being utilized for high-impact was seen when Captain "Sully" Sullenberger capitalized on his years of flying experience and service on accident safety boards to orchestrate the landing of flight 1545 to safety in 2009. A fictional, and more mundane though likely common, example was seen in the 2015 feature film *The Intern*, when Robert De Niro's character used his decades of experience to help his young coworker resolve work-place conflict.

It is important to understand, though, that the rate of these changes within any one particular person will depend on where they were to start, the mosaic of life experiences in and out of work that they have amassed (e.g., at work, in their families), and even their own proactive strategies for aging well (e.g., exercise). All this, mixed in with those larger changes to the work environment we described earlier, creates a complex recipe for change.

So you might be wondering, if there are so many things going that determine how people age, how can I make sense of it all in a way that can be of help? We believe that understanding what we know about how people evolve over their work lives can put people at a tremendous advantage, rather than ignoring the aging of the workforce or simplifying it into generational divisions. Plus, in this book, we couple this knowledge with tools for being able to spot and work with aging employees' specific situations. Moreover, additional tools in this book will help you think like systematically uncover evidence for strategic improvements.

Science-Based Advice Without the Science-Speak

When we set out to write this book, we all believed that it was essential to make science-based advice accessible to everyone, regardless of background. We understand that our readers are very busy and hungry for clear guidance on how best to serve their aging workforce. It is exciting that high-quality scientific research on workforce aging has been growing, but that doesn't do much good if this research is not widely accessible or translatable into action. We are committed to providing science-based advice without the science-speak.

To this end, this book will provide you with accessible, easily understood tools. Throughout the chapters, there are Special Focus Boxes that shine a light on key issues that will help you customize your own solutions for your particular situation, or highlight case studies that bring examples of relevant aging-workforce practices to life (see Special Focus Box 1.2). There are also lists of ideas for action items you can take based on the information in each chapter – with actions you could do right now, in the next week, or in the long term. And for anyone who is curious about the original scientific papers, these resources are provided to you.

Special Focus Box 1.2: Case Study

Cornell University's HR Team Tackles Lifespan Needs in Multiple Ways

Michelle Artibee, MBA, the Director of Workforce Wellbeing in the Division of Human Resources at Cornell, spoke to us about how her team has been working systematically to recognize that flexibility needs change at different life stages and with different life events. Their multipronged approach provides a great model for working to retain talented employees for the long term.

For example:

- Top-down leadership reinforced and encouraged a new perspective. A top leader challenged the HR team to think about all the different ways that the workplace was evolving and how their programming could contribute to a culture of well-being and belonging for all employees across the lifespan.
- More recently, a new HR group was created called Employee Experience. This group brought together existing and new HR professionals that focus on HR analytics, talent management, community embeddedness, work/life, physical health, and mental health. By bringing together these roles, Cornell is better positioned to support employees throughout their lifespan and use a data-informed approach.
- Campus-wide surveys on climate, work/life issues, belongingness, and other concerns – targeting both faculty and staff – provided data to direct and inspire the programming to come.
- They recognize that in Higher Education, faculty often have their identity tied up in their research career (and this is likely the case in many jobs). Previously retirees had often reported that "I don't know who I am anymore" once they retired. Programs that help preretirees with planning and envisioning their future, and creating ways to engage them in the campus and local communities, can help reduce this sense of loss.
- Retaining talent longer means that the odds of disabilities of all sorts may increase. Wellness programming to help support health priorities across the lifespan (e.g., seminars on increasing balance) has been welcome.
- This university is located in a rural area. New faculty (often young, but not necessarily) who arrive without friends, partners, or family can sometimes feel isolated, especially in a town where some families have lived multigenerationally for decades. Programming focusing on

helping younger or other new faculty without local ties feel included and part of the community has become a focus.

- They recognized that their long-standing policy on flexibility in the workplace policy need a major overhaul to keep up with the new culture. First, it was long and daunting, so people were unlikely to become familiar with it. The language in place treated flex as a tool almost exclusively for young working families. This has evolved with the belief that flexibility is a strategic business practice. Childcare is one important issue, but it is not relevant to all employees. There are a lot of other flex needs across the lifespan (e.g., compressed schedules, remote work, and partial-year assignments). The policy was shortened, simplified, edited for potential bias, and provided clear accountability language. All new managers were trained on the meaning and breadth of flexibility.

- Decision-making authority on flex requests from employees still remains with the manager, but prior to issuing any denial to an employee, the manager must discuss their decision with local HR support, who can challenge their thinking and rationale. Clear performance management discussions are encouraged.

- Highly skilled benefits counselors are available to talk about all kinds of life transitions after a robust overhaul of the benefits customer service model. They are well equipped to guide faculty and staff navigating life events such as divorce, major illness, or adoption, to name a few. This sends a message they are dedicated to helping people throughout the life cycle.

- Expanding the notion of well-being beyond just physical well-being allowed for more diverse thinking as to how to help increase well-being for all employees, regardless of age and other lifestyle factors.

- Even after retirement, there are programs to keep retirees involved in the University and ambassador opportunities so they can help newly retired individuals and work at various events and activities.

The PIERA Framework

One unique feature worthy of mention here is the guiding framework we use throughout the book, called PIERA. This acronym stands for Plan, Implement, Evaluate, Reflect, and Adjust. No ideas work the same for all people and situations, and even if we make suggestions that are based on sound evidence, you need to be sure it will work for you in your situation. The PIERA framework provides guidance on how to wisely approach the implementation of new ideas. This will be useful to you not only for trying out the information based on this book, but also for testing any type of new strategy you'd like to try to improve your workplace. We devote the next chapter to the details of the PIERA approach.

Action Items: Things to Do Right Now, Next Week, Long Term

Right Now

Before you put down this book, take the next five minutes or so to write down one issue you face at work that you think this book might be able to help you with. Look over the Table of Contents and note which chapters might be the most relevant to you.

Next Week

Schedule some time on your calendar over the next week to really dive into this book – scheduling in reading time helps it happen. When can you grab some coffee or tea and find a quiet place to read and reflect?

Long Term

Think about how generational stereotypes work their way into your workplace. Do people discuss the generations as if they are different species, and if everyone from a certain generation thinks and acts alike? Moving forward, think about different ways you can help redirect this kind of misguided thinking when it comes up.

Notes

1. Finkelstein, L. M., Truxillo, D.T., Fraccaroli, F., & Kanfer, R. (2015). An introduction to facing the challenges of a multi-age workforce: A use-inspired approach. In L. Finkelstein, D. Truxillo, F. Fraccaroli, & R. Kanfer (Eds.), *Facing the challenges of a multi-age workforce: A use-inspired approach* (pp. 3–22.). New York, NY: Routledge.
2. Costanza, D. P., & Finkelstein, L. M. (2017). Generationally-based differences in the workplace: Is there a there there? *Industrial and Organizational Psychology, 8*, 308–323.

3. Costanza, D., Finkelstein, L. M., Imose, R. A., & Ravid, D. M. (2020). Inappropriate inferences from generational research. In B. J. Hoffman, M.K. Shoss, & L. A. Wegman (Eds.), *The Cambridge handbook of the changing nature of work* (pp. 20–41). Cambridge, UK: Cambridge University Press.

4. National Academies of Sciences, Engineering, and Medicine. (2020). *Are generational categories meaningful distinctions for workforce management?* Washington, DC: The National Academies Press. https://doi.org/10.17226/25796.

5. Giannakouris, K. (2008). Ageing characterises the demographic perspectives of the European societies. *Eurostat Statistics in Focus, 72.* Available at: http://epp.eurostat.ec.europa.eu/cahe/ITY_OFFPUB/KS-SF-08-072/EN/KS-SF-08-072-EN.pdf

6. U.S. Bureau of Labor Statistics Occupational Outlook Handbook. Available at: https://www.bls.gov/ooh/healthcare/home.htm

7. Finkelstein et al. (2015).

8. Czaja, S. J., Charness, N., Fisk, A. D., Hertzog, C., Nair, S. N., Rogers, W. A., & Sharit, J. (2006). Factors predicting the use of technology: Findings from the center for research and education on aging and technology enhancement (CREATE). *Psychology and Aging, 21, 333–352.*

9. Barber, L. K., & Santuzzi, A. M. (2015). Please respond ASAP: Workplace telepressure and employee recovery. *Journal of Occupational Health Psychology, 20, 172–189.*

10. Finkelstein et al. (2015).

11. Baldwin, R. (2019). *The globotics upheaval: Globalization, robotics, and the future of work.* Oxford, UK: Oxford University Press.

12. Park, D. C., & Reuter-Lorenz, P. (2009). The adaptive brain: Aging and neurocognitive scaffolding. *Annual Review of Psychology, 60, 173–196.*

13. Scheibe, S., & Carstensen, L. L. (2010). Emotional aging: Recent findings and future trends. *Journal of Gerontology: Psychological Sciences, 65B, 135–144.*

The PIERA Approach and How to Use It   **2**

In Chapter 1 we introduced the idea of the PIERA approach. In this chapter, we flesh out this idea to explain what the PIERA steps are and why they are necessary. We provide some suggestions for how you can use PIERA to make real and sustainable changes in your work environment that improve the workplace for employees of all ages.

As we described in the last chapter, organizations that prosper are organizations that learn and grow. PIERA describes the proactive process by which organizations and the people in them adapt to new contingencies and develop new strategies for success. In this chapter, we provide you with tools to help you master the challenges associated with managing a diverse and ever-changing human workforce. We describe how to apply and teach these tools to other leaders in your organization as well.

We begin by spending some time on this idea of a learning organization – what exactly does it entail? Is your organization already a learning organization? We'll draw from the research in this area, including the idea that organizational buy-in from the top will make this whole operation go much more smoothly. We'll provide you with some tools to help you build this solid support structure as you take on the PIERA challenge.

What Is PIERA?

A Learning Organization

Although all organizations are made up of people, and all people learn things on a pretty continuous basis whether they realize it or not, not all organizations can be characterized as learning organizations. Learning organizations are those that embody a positive mindset that holds that all members have the mission and the ability to continually and proactively acquire new knowledge that is helpful to the organization, to share and distribute this knowledge, and to actually translate it and put it to use where it is most needed.[1] Members of the organization develop a shared viewpoint (what's often called a shared mental model) of what the organization stands for, what it does, and how it functions.[2]

Sounds like a great idea, right? But in order for it to actually work – for employees and teams to know how to do this *and* to be motivated to do this – certain structures need to be in place. For the first part of this process, the organizational learning component, it must be clearly communicated from all levels of leadership that continuous learning is both expected and rewarded, and incentives must be in place to encourage it. If you tell your employees that they should be learning and innovating beyond the structured training and development activities provided by the organization, but then give them no time or resources to do so, it is unlikely to happen with any regularity.

Organizations with a learning culture share knowledge openly and broadly. But how does this happen? It requires both social and technological infrastructure. Socially, if the organization is ruled by intense internal competition among employees or departments, why would anyone want to give away their "secret sauce" to a colleague? Any impression of a political minefield within the organization can stifle widespread information sharing.[3] Employees need to be able to see how sharing knowledge benefits them personally if the organization as a whole is to improve its performance and standing through shared knowledge. Human resource systems, like performance appraisals, that track and reward knowledge acquisition and sharing as a valued aspect of individual employee performance, send a message that sharing knowledge helps the individual's own career outlook as well as the organization's performance. Supervisors also play a crucial role in letting employees know that their collaboration with others is valued by the organization. As research shows, recognition from one's boss is a powerful incentive for increasing any behavior – including knowledge sharing and collaboration. Further, if managers want to increase knowledge sharing, they need to model it themselves and actively foster a culture that supports it.

Sometimes, one of the best ways to learn is to learn what *doesn't* work; mistakes are part of the innovation process. If a culture does not have room for experimentation and safe failures, learning will be stunted. Top leaders of learning organizations actively walk the talk of knowledge seeking, experimentation, and reflecting and resetting the course of action after a setback. If there is threat associated with embarrassment, or fear of repercussions from not succeeding right out of the box on the first try at something new, proper methods for course correcting may be never be learned.[4]

Finally, effective knowledge sharing among employees requires a supportive technological infrastructure. Organizational information systems vary, but should minimally include platforms that allow employees to upload knowledge and seek out the most updated knowledge, and these should be broadly and easily accessible throughout all levels of the organization. Additional forms of knowledge sharing may include podcasts and blogs. Additionally, actual physical spaces where people are encouraged to interact regularly, and work designs that allow for and encourage open idea sharing within and across levels are important low-tech prongs in the infrastructure.[5] Top leaders who ask workers how and why they do what they do and really listen can send a message that curiosity and respect for diverse perspectives is valued.[6]

How does being part of a learning organization foster the ideas we present in this book? You'll see that our PIERA framework encourages systematic learning, experimentation, evaluation, and reflection on a small scale to test out some of the successful ideas that are provided here. What's more, we will encourage you to share the specifics about what you are learning, as well this PIERA framework as a whole, with others throughout your organization. A learning organization structure encourages these types of procedures – in fact, if you've been embedded in this kind of organization for a while this type of strategy is probably not entirely new to you.

So, what if you believe that your organization doesn't quite fill the bill as a learning organization? Are you out of luck? Definitely not! But it will be important to keep this potential challenge in mind as you proceed and to clearly communicate to your leaders, direct reports, and those affected by your change intervention the specifics of what you are trying out and why you believe it is important. We've provided an example tool in Special Focus Box 2.1 to help you determine the degree to which yours is a learning organization, and another in Special Focus Box 2.2 with

Special Focus Box 2.1: Are You a Part of a Learning Organization?

Researchers David Garvin, Amy Edmundson, and Francesca Gino have developed a tool to help give you an idea of how well the features of your organization maps on to the features of a Learning Organization. After you complete the survey, benchmarking information is provided. Getting an idea of where your organization stands can help determine the ease at which you are likely to be able to implement the ideas in this book.

To access this survey, go to los.hbs.edu.

Special Focus Box 2.2: Getting Leader Support for Your Intervention Ideas

Organizational scholars Susan Ashford and James Detert share their ideas about getting leadership buy-in for your ideas in an hbr.org article that can be found here: https://hbr.org/2015/01/get-the-boss-to-buy-in. We encourage you to check this out, but here is a brief summary of their tips:

1. Tailor your message specifically to the goals and values of the person you are approaching. Think about what part of your ideas align best with those goals and emphasize that.
2. Package your ideas to make the business benefits as clear as possible.
3. Pay attention to regulating strong emotions. This includes yours (don't come across as coming from a place of anger and frustration) and those of your audience (read reactions and adjust course as needed).
4. Plan your timing. What's going on not only in your organization but also in the world that speaks to the benefits of your ideas?
5. Get others on your side. Can you rally allies in the organization (who are trusted by leaders) for your idea before pitching it?
6. Know the norms. Having a grasp of expected behaviors and communication channels in your organization can keep you from stepping on toes before even getting off the ground.
7. Raise solutions, not just problems. Come to the table not only with an idea of what should be improved but some feasible ways to improve it.

some helpful pointers to use to approach stakeholders to garner support for your endeavors.

Components of PIERA

Even in a learning organization that promotes ongoing learning, change, and improvement, there are times when an unexpected turn of events or even a crisis can hit, requiring resilience and new ways of approaching work.[7] For example, as we've mentioned, we are wrapping up the writing of this book in the midst of the COVID-19 pandemic. Although the PIERA method can be used when considering any change – urgent or not – it may prove to be an especially useful tool when the importance of responsiveness to change is paramount.

Do you remember what we told you PIERA stands for? Planning, Implementation, Evaluation, Reflection, and Adjustment. Each of these elements is an important part of the small-scale experimentation to use with the ideas presented in this book. Let's take a closer look at these steps.

Planning

The first and arguably most crucial stage of any kind of change at work is the planning stage. Planning involves three elements. First, you need to have a specific goal or outcome in mind so you know where you are going. What are you trying to accomplish? Second, planning requires that you conduct a diagnosis of the current situation so you can know where you are starting from. For example, what are the symptoms that there might be a problem? After understanding what you want to achieve and where you are currently, the last step in this stage is to generate a plan for how you are going to get from the present to the desired future state – what you might implement to address the problems you have uncovered. Effective planning requires all three elements.

If you are thinking of trying out a strategy described in this book, we encourage you to take a good look at your current situation to figure out if it is a good fit. Something might sound like an interesting idea, but if it focuses on something that isn't problematic in your workplace, there is no need to proceed. For example, having older workers mentor junior colleagues is a great way to nurture new hires and increase older worker engagement, but not if people are feeling that they can't keep up with their current work.

What is the goal of your strategy tryout? How will accomplishing the goal improve or mitigate problems in your workplace? After reading through the book, it will be helpful to investigate where your organizational challenges are, or where you could do just a little bit more to improve your focus on employee's changing needs and talents over time. Having open dialogue with those in your work environment, through discussions or even anonymous surveys, can help reveal blind spots. Including other stakeholders in the planning stage could generate support or even excitement over the potential for positive change.

Maybe you have an idea you'd like to try out in your organization. It would generally address a need you have, but the details don't quite fit your environment. Planning is needed to help you translate your idea into a goal that fits within your culture, and involves change in your employee's behavior that is within their scope. Planning is not implementation, but rather thinking through what is involved in implementation and getting prepared before it happens.[8] For example, people in most positions would likely need some permission from those above to try out a new strategy; having a clear written plan in place should increase the likelihood that this would go smoothly.

Implementation

This is where you get to try your plan out – the fun and potentially slightly scary part of any endeavor! Implementation is a trial run or an experiment of sorts – where you make a change for a specified and bounded period of time with a subset of people. Small-scale implementation is a lower risk strategy that allows you to see how your plan works and how employees respond to the plan so that you can refine your plan before instituting it on a larger scale where the stakes are higher. Regardless of the size of the implementation, clear communication with everyone involved and careful monitoring of the processes is critical. Few plans work without hiccups, and the purpose of implementing on a small scale is to identify potential people and strategy problems early so you can fix them in subsequent runs. Implementation is often when you learn the most about your organization and the barriers to achieving your goals. At this stage, you may need to revise your plan or brainstorm ways to overcome unanticipated obstacles. At the same time, implementation may be very motivating and engender higher levels of team trust, as people work together for a specific goal.

Evaluation

Obviously, you will be eager to know how your trial went. But how will you know if you are successful? Before rushing to collect some data to determine how your change worked, first you need to know what "worked" looks like. Identify what success will look like and how you will measure it *before* you implement your plan. Once you know have a vision of what success will look like, it is easier to determine the best measurement instruments to use and the right people to use them with. Also, we're often interested not only in the end result but in how smoothly the process went along the way. That means there is a need for not only evaluating what happened *resulting* from your trial program, but also for thinking systematically about how behaviors and reactions *unfolded* over the course of the trial to more deeply understand what led to change.[9] This information may prove valuable in future change attempts as well.

Although a deep dive into program evaluation methods is beyond the scope of this book, we will provide examples of evaluation ideas throughout the book, along with resources for those who want further information. As a start, check out Special Focus Box 2.3.

Special Focus Box 2.3: Evaluating a Trial Intervention: Questions to Consider

- Were you realistic in the goal you wanted to achieve?
- Did you focus on the correct behaviors you wanted to change to accomplish the goal?
- Might there be another more realistic goal?
- Were you realistic in the level of skill and readiness your employees had for implementing this trial?
- How would you evaluate the adequacy of your plan? Was the goal clear to everyone involved?
- Was the plan for how to achieve the outcome doable with the time and resources involved?
- Did people enjoy working toward the goals during implementation?
- What do you now realize you forgot when making your plan?
- Do you believe you were able to accurately measure the change that took place?
- Do you have sufficient information about what might be changed in your intervention?

Reflection

All too often, people make snap judgments about whether a plan worked based on a single indicator. Given the time and effort you and your colleagues have put into this process, it makes sense that you take time to think and talk about the experience, the ways that changes occurred, and the reasons for the outcomes you observed. Did you get the change you wanted? If not, why not? Did you get changes you didn't anticipate? Why do you think that occurred? How much would the needle have to move on that gauge for you to believe the plan was successful enough to keep up or even expand the change? Did everything proceed and turn out as planned, or were there bumps along the road? All of these questions, and possibly others more tailored to your own situation, are a crucial part of the reflection process.

The act of critically reflecting after feedback and taking time to really think about what happened and why it happened is something that is supported by science in many different realms – from the Army's After Action Reviews[10] to studies on education[11] and performance appraisals.[12] This is sometimes easier said than done because it can be hard to hear (or read) less-than-stellar feedback on something that you've put effort into. There are a couple of helpful things to remember here. First, remember that this was just a try-out. Anything that didn't work provides information to get you one step closer to something that will fit better. Second, remember that "critical" reflection doesn't mean criticizing the person who tried out an idea; rather, it means *thinking constructively about what went right or wrong in the specific situation as the idea was implemented.*

Reflection is best done not in isolation but with others who can help ask probing questions and provide divergent perspectives. Allowing others to be open and forthcoming in this process is essential, and in some organizational cultures where politeness above all else is the norm this could prove difficult.[13] If done well, this collective process can also assist with in the final step of PIERA – taking what has been learned and figuring out where to go next.

Adjustment

After your honest, clearheaded, and nonjudgmental reflection on the results of your experiment, what's next? What should be adjusted before you proceed? Are there only slight tweaks required, or does your experiment constitute one of those in the "knowing what doesn't work is learning too" column? Here you make this determination and begin the next PIERA cycle until you (and your stakeholders) are satisfied and can institutionalize, and perhaps expand, the change into new strategy or policy throughout the organization as needed.

PIERA and This Book

You now have the basic idea of the principles involved in the PIERA system. Each of the remaining chapters in the book focuses on a specific aspect of work where a deeper understanding of workers as they age can inspire positive change. These aspects range from interpersonal interactions across age groups, to worker well-being, to learning and development strategies…the list goes on. Although we have provided some general guidance for PIERA in this chapter, in the chapters to follow, we will highlight some examples of how PIERA could be applied to test out an intervention pertinent to the workplace topic at hand. Specific examples will help bring this to life. Let's start with one here.

PIERA in Action

For our example, let's think about the tricky and ubiquitous issue of work-life balance (to be explored more deeply in Chapter 7). Consider the situation where an organization has some standardized flextime policy that's available when employees need time for childcare or eldercare issues. There may also be telecommuting options in place for certain types of jobs; for jobs where telecommuting was possible, this became a mandate and not a choice for many workers at least for a time during the height of the COVID-19 pandemic. A manager may notice that workers are complaining about being pulled in too many directions and of being overwhelmed. Is there more that could be done with these policies? And could the organization go beyond policy, in terms of supporting managers or departments who are working through these issues?

Additionally, do the issues that surround work-life balance differ systematically for employees of different ages? That is, are there different types of obligations outside of work for older and younger people? Also, does it depend on the individual life stage, circumstance, preference, and personality of each employee? How can one determine the best place to start to make a difference in the work-life balance perceptions now for as many employees as possible, do it fairly, and ensure a dynamism that can continue to help employees as they transition to various work and life roles over time?

You notice that there are a few different approaches to addressing work-life balance in organizations. For example, some organizations focus on implementing policies that allow for flexible work times and locations – and this has been shown to affect older workers' desire to continue working.[14] Other approaches go a step farther than just the policy and involve teaching the supervisor to support employees' work-life balance and to model a balanced lifestyle themselves; this intervention seems to affect outcomes from well-being to sleep.[15] Which of these, if any, or in what form, might work in your organization?

Enter PIERA. Each chapter will end with an example us of the PIERA method or a set of guiding questions that can be applied toward one or more example interventions that had been described in the chapter. This will provide a touchstone for the steps involved to adapt an idea from the book to your workplace in an actionable way. See below.

PIERA Example: The PIERA Approach to a Work-Life Balance Intervention

Planning

- Is work-life balance currently a struggle for the people in your department? How do you know it is a problem? What are the symptoms of a problem, for example, do workers or their managers verbalize this concern? What outcomes do you think this problem affects? For example, does it affect employee attitudes, retention, absenteeism, team performance, unit performance?
- Who is affected by this problem? Is it people of all ages, or only certain groups? Is this a problem that everyone seems to experience, or is it a problem more related to the employee's circumstances (e.g., men/women; younger/older; certain positions)? If it is a single group, is there a solution that is fair to all workers? For example, a program that helps people with small children but puts more stress on other workers is not likely to succeed.
- What is your specific goal here? What specific issue are you trying to change or improve?
- What is the current policy on work-life balance? How do you know it is coming up short?

- What is the culture regarding work-life balance in your organization? Do managers across the board tend to support it and model it?
- In what ways do the example interventions above – and they are only examples – apply to your situation, and how might they need to be adapted? Would you use some combination of interventions?
- Are the problems and symptoms you've uncovered truly related to work-life balance or to other issues?
- If you implement some changes to address work-life balance, how will you measure success during your trial period? Will you use surveys? Interviews? Key informants? Remember, if the solution that you originally implemented is not solving the problems or is causing others, it is important to find out and change course during the "reflection" stage, below.
- What strategy for implementing your program will you use, and how will you deal with any problem situations that you might encounter?

Implementation

- It's time to put your plan into action. Make sure everyone involved is clear on what will be happening and when.
- Are there any warning signs of problems? Does anyone involved seemed to be confused about their role?
- Do you sense any resistance? For example, does one group of employees seem to feel that this benefits only others and so is unfair?
- If top management had expressed support for a change, are they demonstrating that support during the intervention?
- Is anything not playing out as planned? Does anything need changing?

Evaluation

- What behaviors and performance changed as a result of the intervention?
- What behaviors and performance did NOT change?
- What were the employee attitudes toward the change?
- Any systematic measurement (survey, focus groups, etc.) that you do should be focused on the purposes you determined in the planning stage. Be sure your measurement really gets at what you want to know. There may be surveys that already exist and are available for widespread use. For example, some statements (to which people rate their agreement) used in a Family Supportive Supervisor Scale[16] include things like "I can rely on my supervisor to make sure my work responsibilities are handled when I have unanticipated nonwork issues" and "My supervisor demonstrates effective behaviors in how to juggle work and nonwork balance".

Reflection

- Was the strategy effective in mitigating the problem?
- What changes could be made to:
  - Change the content or focus of the intervention?
  - Change the process by which the intervention was implemented?

Adjustment

- How will you actually implement and evaluate the program on a larger scale?
- What changes will you need to make before doing so?
- Is there anything you would do differently, either in the intervention itself or in its implementation in the organization (e.g., communication with employees about why it is being done)?

Notes

1. Cummings, T. J., & Worley, C. G. (2009). *Organizational development & change* (9th ed.). Mason, OH: South-Western Cengage Learning.
2. Bui, H., & Baruch, Y. (2010). Creating learning organizations: A systems perspective. *The Learning Organization, 17,* 208–227.
3. Serrat, O. (2017). *Knowledge solutions.* Singapore: Springer Open.
4. Ibid.
5. Ibid.
6. Garvin, D. G., Edmondson, A. C., & Gino, F. (2008). Is yours a learning organization? *Harvard Business Review, 86,* 109–116.
7. Weick, K. E., & Sutcliffe, K. M. (2007). *Managing the unexpected: Resilient performance in an age of uncertainty* (2nd ed.). San Francisco, CA: Jossey-Bass.
8. Cummings and Worley (2009).
9. Biron, C., & Karanika-Murray, M. (2013). Process evaluation for organizational stress and well-being interventions: Implications for theory, research, and practice. *International Journal of Stress Management, 21,* 85–111.
10. Morrison, J. E., & Meliza, L. L. (1999). Foundations of the after action review process. U. S. Army Research Institute for the Behavioral and Social Sciences, Special Report No. 42.
11. Closs, L. & Antonello, C. S. (2011). Transformative learning: Integrating critical reflection into management education. *Journal of Transformative Education, 9,* 63–88.

12. Anseel, F., Lievens, F., & Schollaert, E. (2009). Reflection as a strategy to enhance performance after feedback. *Organizational Behavior and Human Decision Processes, 110,* 23–35.

13. Brooks, A. K. (1999). Critical reflection as a response to organizational disruption. *Advances in Developing Human Resources, 1,* 66–79.

14. Cahill, K. E., James, J. B., & Pitt-Catsouphes, M. (2015). The impact of a randomly assigned time and place management initiative on work and retirement expectations. *Work, Aging and Retirement, 1*(4), 350–368.

15. Hammer, L. B., Truxillo, D. M., Bodner, T., Pytlovany, A. C., & Richman, A. (2019). Exploration of the impact of organisational context on a workplace safety and health intervention. *Work & Stress, 33*(2), 192–210.

16. Hammer, L. B., Kossek, E. E., Bodner, T. E., & Hanson, G. C. (2009). Development and validation of a multidimensional measure of family supportive supervisor behaviors (FSSB). *Journal of Management, 35,* 837–856.

Motivation and Engagement Across the Working Lifetime

3

This chapter is about employee motivation and engagement. It is not about presenting you with one "right way" to motivate your employees, but rather about helping you understand how motivation and engagement work, the tools at your disposal, and providing you with suggestions for when you might use them. Building and maintaining employee motivation is one of the most complex tasks that leaders and managers undertake. Different employees respond to different strategies, and increasing age diversity adds to this complexity. Some employees respond very well to changes you make in how well you listen to them and support their accomplishments. Others may not respond to those changes much, but rather become energized and engaged by the things you do that help them see their work in a different light (e.g., as helping others), or the changes you make in their work role that better suit their changing interests and talents. In this chapter, we also discuss how employee aging and life stage can affect work motivation and engagement. Using our PIERA approach this chapter aims to give you insights to help strengthen your skills as an effective, engaging manager.

What Is Work Motivation?

Everyone has a different idea of what motivation is. Scientific definitions emphasize that motivation is an energizing process – people work harder and persist longer when motivated. Scientific definitions also highlight the emergent quality of motivation, as a force that arises as a consequence of an individual's interactions with people and the work environment.[1] Although we understand that motivation can't be directly measured, most of us feel that we know it when we see it. That is because we are making an inference about an employee's behavior based on what we know about the employee and the situation. For example, we may infer that an employee who occasionally turns her work in late on an exciting, important project lacks motivation and commitment. But we can't be sure. Her poor performance may be due to her preoccupation with caring for a sick mother. Inferences about why an employee lacks motivation and is performing poorly are often not correct.

Similarly, we are often more confident about our inferences of high motivation (e.g., an employee who stays late to finish a boring task). Again, however, what drives the employee's behavior may not be what you think it is (e.g., the employee may be more interested in striking up a relationship with another coworker staying late rather than finishing the boring task). Whether we are making inferences of poor or excellent work motivation, we need to be cautious and learn more about the employee and the work context before we make judgments. In the following sections, we describe the key levers in work motivation and engagement.

Motivation for What?

At first glance, this may seem like a silly question. But in fact, it turns out to be a difficult one that lies at the heart of good people management. Think about what motivates you. You can probably tick off many things. The nature of your job – managing others – may satisfy needs for being social and helping others. You may work hard and come up with creative solutions to problems in part to be noticed by your boss, and hopefully to be rewarded with a pay increase and / or development opportunities. You may work long hours in part because your life situation allows it, and you might be energized by anticipating the pride you will feel when you achieve challenging performance goals. You may work diligently at your job because you like where you work and the organization. And finally, some of your motivation may derive from the respect you have for your boss and your desire to help her achieve the team's goal. Obviously, what drives employee motivation and task persistence is certainly not one thing. It is a set of needs, interests, beliefs, feelings, goals, and life situations that differ across people and over time. It varies not only depending on an employee's talents, personality, and interests but also on how that individual is energized by his work role, the work environment, and the people around him.

One way to get a handle on the "for what" question is to distinguish between intrinsic and extrinsic rewards and motivation. Intrinsic and extrinsic motivation differ depending on whether the reason for the behavior is driven by satisfying our psychological self (intrinsic motivation) or by obtaining (or even avoiding) an external outcome (extrinsic motivation). Examples of outcomes associated with intrinsic motivation include pride in one's work, a sense of belonging in the group, feelings of skill mastery and job competence, feelings of control or autonomy, and/or feelings of purpose or meaningfulness in one's work. Examples of outcomes associated with extrinsic motivation include pay, promotions, and perks. Extrinsic rewards have long been the main way by which organizations have recruited, motivated, and retained employees. Companies in the competitive high tech world, for example, may provide benefits such as on-site dry cleaning, fitness programs, or free food at work as extrinsic inducements for recruits to join their organization. Once onboard, extrinsic rewards such as contingent bonus pay, perks, flexible work policies, promotions, and development opportunities may be implemented to support employee motivation. In general, supervisors use extrinsic rewards (beyond regular pay) to increase work motivation in specific circumstances, such as when trying to persuade an employee to enroll in new skill training, to develop an innovative product, or to remain with the company. Extrinsic rewards are also useful when supervisors want to spur a burst of greater effort among experienced workers (competition) for a limited period of time.

In contrast, intrinsic motivation pertains to thoughts, feelings, and the sense of well-being associated with motivation at work. Although intrinsic outcomes occur within the individual, organizations and supervisors play an important role in creating the conditions that promote intrinsic work motivation. Most employees, for example, want to feel a sense of belonging in their unit or team. Organizational norms and supervisory actions can promote intrinsic motivation by signaling to the employee that she adds value to the unit, regardless of age and ethnicity. Supervisors can also enhance intrinsic motivation by working with the employee to revise or craft the employee's job in more meaningful ways.[2] For example, among employees who highly value teaching or assisting others (as often occurs among midcareer employees), supervisors may amend the work role to include mentoring of a younger employee or an opportunity to teach the team a skill. Yet other supervisory actions can enhance intrinsic motivation by arranging work into a more integral set of activities or arranging for employees to see the importance of their work. For example, supervisors in a medical supply plant might have healthcare providers visit or write letters that convey how the employee's job affects their work. Intrinsic motivation is a deeply powerful motivator. Employees who experience intrinsic motivation often report that they enjoy their work, and are more likely to work longer at the job than employees who feel little sense of control, or value in their work role.

For most people, work involves a mix of extrinsic and intrinsic motivations. An award that provides extra pay for excellent performance provides both a feeling of pride (a source of intrinsic motivation) and an extrinsic reward (pay). Over the course of a career, the influence of intrinsic and extrinsic rewards to stimulate motivation can change. For example, for new lawyers entering a practice, extrinsic rewards (related to pay and promotion opportunities available for excellent work) loom large in the reason for working long, late hours. Over time, however, these long hours, often result in new skill learning and the development of social relationships that, in turn, promote intrinsic motivation through feelings of belonging (professional identity), competence, and control. That is, intrinsic motives often take a larger role in powering work motivation as job experience increases.

Among mid-to-late career employees, for example, the most salient and motivating aspect of earning a one-time performance bonus is not the few hundred dollars of extra income, but the public recognition and pride associated with receiving the award. Although some people say that they work just for the pay, and others that they work just for the love of the work, few employees are motivated for one or the other exclusively. Creating an engaged workforce requires balancing the mix of extrinsic/intrinsic rewards in ways that allows employees to find opportunities for well-being in the work they perform, to feel respected by others, and to feel fairly valued (paid) for their talents and efforts.

We have argued that extrinsic rewards can also provide intrinsic outcomes that fuel employee motivation. However, the use of extrinsic rewards, such as bonus pay, can also have serious drawbacks. The frequent use of extrinsic rewards (beyond pay) in which the reward is very salient can be interpreted by employees as controlling and "crowd out" or reduce intrinsic motivation.[3] That is, employees can come to view their motivation as driven by the extrinsic reward rather than as a sense of self-determination. Finally, some extrinsic rewards that are tied to performance metrics may not be related to employee motivation at all, and can actually demotivate employees! For example, offering a monthly bonus to the real-estate sales team with the highest dollar sales figure for the month may be demotivating to team members whose territory covers lower cost homes. Caution should be used when introducing extrinsic rewards beyond pay, particularly if the reward has the potential for undermining intrinsic motivation.

An oft-used, practical alternative is to use "soft" extrinsic rewards, such as supervisor or peer support or praise. These "extrinsic" rewards, typically administered by you or others in the unit, build intrinsic work motivation. Numerous studies show that when employees feel confident and self-determining, they report higher engagement and more positive work attitudes.[4] Soft extrinsic rewards are also quite important for preventing demotivation. Employees who perceive little control over or effect on their work situation may reduce their motivation and, over time, and exhibit a "learned helplessness" profile in which they stop taking the initiative when problems arise.

For example, one of the authors has a friend we will call Jacob. Jacob worked for many years as a governmental procurement officer. Although he was an energetic and proactive individual in early adulthood, the hierarchical and rigid nature of his work role required that he report rather than resolve procurement problems, and that he wait for a solution from his supervisor. Further, the organizational norm was to accept but not praise good work. Over the years, the lack of self-determination in his job discouraged him and spilled over to increasing passivity in his nonwork life. He retired as soon as he was eligible to receive a pension. Although no employee is completely self-determining, soft extrinsic rewards can powerfully increase feelings of self-determination and work motivation. Supervisors can also increase an employee's feeling of self-determination by listening to employee concerns and recommendations, helping to improve work role fit (e.g., increasing schedule flexibility), and including the employee in discussions about important aspects of unit and organizational life.

What's Age Got to Do with Motivation?

It is a popular but erroneous stereotype that work motivation declines with age.[5] Among older people performing intrinsically satisfying jobs, work motivation may actually increase with age. In our own research, we found that CEOs, who typically enjoy high levels of autonomy, report significantly later retirement intentions than employees. For some employees, work motivation may decline with age as retirement savings and nonwork and leisure activities provide attractive extrinsic and intrinsic options. For other older employees with strong financial needs and little in retirement savings, work motivation may be propelled by job insecurity and the fear of losing their job. And for other older employees, work motivation may decline as younger employees are hired and the sense of belongingness at work wanes. The point is that age-related changes in work motivation are not necessarily negative or due solely to growing older per se.

An important factor in age-related changes in work motivation stems from the extent to which the work role continues to fit with an employee's changing needs, goals, and interests. Research shows that younger employees tend to more strongly value extrinsic rewards such as opportunities for skill training and career advancement. In contrast, mid-to-late career employees often more highly value work roles that allow them to utilize their existing skills, and to maximize job security.[6] Late-career workers report higher value for jobs that allow the use of well-developed skills, and work roles that fit their changing profile of resources. Understanding the basis for age-related changes in work motives is described in more detail later in this chapter. Knowing these reasons for age-related differences further helps to understand what strategies and reward combinations will likely be most appealing and motivating to which employees. Why, for example, might a late-career employee be less likely to be motivated by the promise of a promotion than an early-career employee, but more motivated by the opportunity to coach younger employees?

What Is Employee Engagement?

Many people assume that motivation and engagement are the same thing. They are related, but they are not the same thing. Motivation is about getting an individual to devote more of their attention to a task, work harder, and persist longer. But motivation is only one part of the larger bundle of thoughts, feelings, and behaviors that make up employee engagement.

Engaged employees are dedicated, find enjoyment and challenge in their work, believe that their work is important, and allocate high levels of effort and performance even when faced with setbacks. Beyond work motivation, engaged employees often work hard in part out of a felt commitment to help accomplish an organization's goals. Engaged employees often share the same goals as their organization or unit. They exert effort not just for the rewards associated with personal success, but for the intrinsic and extrinsic rewards associated with seeing their unit or organization succeed.[7] In many modern organizations, the manager's goal is not just to motivate employees, but to build employee engagement. Research findings show that engagement can be increased by improving the employee's capabilities and well-being, including feelings of work involvement, self-esteem, and the experience of positive emotions.[8] Increasing employee engagement (rather than focusing exclusively on work motivation) is an effective means of enhancing employee performance, particularly among late-career employees.

Now that you understand the basics of motivation and engagement, let's take stock of how you currently use resources at your disposal to motivate and engage your employees. Special Focus Box 3.1 contains examples of rewards and strategies managers routinely use to enhance

Special Focus Box 3.1: Examples of Managerial Strategies to Enhance Employee Motivation and Engagement

- Offer a bonus for achieving a performance goal
- Set clear, specific realistic work goals
- Provide employees with formative feedback
- Work with an employee to overcome a performance problem
- Talk with employees about the value of their job to the unit and organization
- Praise an employee for task effort and persistence
- Include employees in discussions about ways to improve teamwork
- Share inspirational information and stories
- Pair young-old employees to provide dual, two-way mentoring
- Explain and discuss with employees why changes are being made
- Empower employees to make their own decisions when possible
- Choose your words and rewards carefully to let employees know they count
- Foster a climate of personal safety for employees
- Clarify the organization's mission and values
- Adjust an employee's job to accommodate short-term illness or disability

Special Focus Box 3.2: Reflecting on Your Motivational Style

1. How would you describe your strategy profile? Are you more prone to using extrinsic or intrinsic/soft extrinsic reward strategies?
2. Do you use the same strategies with all your employees, or different strategies for which employees? Do you prefer to motivate employees one-on-one or the team as a whole?
3. Which strategies are you most comfortable using? Least comfortable? Why?

motivation and engagement. How many of these strategies do you use? Special Focus Box 3.2 contains a brief exercise to help you reflect on your strategy profile. How broad and varied is your repertoire for motivating employees? Do you focus more on extrinsic, intrinsic, or mixed motivational strategies? How do you choose which strategy to use when?

Putting What We Know about Motivation and Engagement into Practice

As we noted before, people are rarely maximally motivated or completely unmotivated – changes in motivation and engagement occur along a continuum and over time. Changes in how much effort we devote to a task often changes moment-by-moment and day-by-day, and depends on many things, such as our emotions, what else is happening, and the task.[9] Reflect on your own experience for a moment and think about how your work motivation might change within a single workday, or across the work week. Things that could affect your motivation for even a short time include, for example, how much sleep, food, or coffee you have had, frustrations you had getting into an online meeting, a positive interaction you had with a coworker or your supervisor, or the extent to which you were preoccupied with a nonwork issue, such as a sick child. Whether you are an energetic person in general or not, your work motivation will vary quite a bit over any given week.

Similar to work motivation, employee engagement also varies over time. But in contrast to work motivation, engagement tends to vary over a longer time cycle. Aerospace engineers who are challenged by difficult work problems, such as how to get to improve spaceship design, often work long hours and report high levels of engagement. Engagement is also affected by the people that an employee works with and for. Members of a paramedic ambulance team for example work together for many hours each day and often become highly dedicated to helping each other and being a successful team. Mid- and late-career employees who have developed strong positive relationships over the years with colleagues across the company also often report high levels of dedication to the organization.

At the same time, employees can also experience a decline in engagement as a result of social and work conditions. Following the pandemic, mass layoffs in the hospitality industry created additional workloads and increased job insecurity that weakened job engagement as surviving employees sought new, more secure jobs. Among older employees, lack of supervisory support and respect by one's supervisor may reduce engagement and strengthen retirement intentions. Because higher levels of employee engagement typically spur higher levels of work motivation and enhanced well-being, managers have increasingly focused on enhancing employee engagement rather than just work motivation.

One important way that organizational personnel and supervisors can enhance employee engagement and motivation is by adjusting the employee's working experience. When using this strategy, however, it is important to take into account age-related differences in what makes for an optimal, challenging work experience – a job that is neither too boring nor too difficult. For example, early-career employees often enjoy jobs that involve the frequent introduction of new work routines and technologies that provide new learning opportunities. Among older workers, however, jobs with these characteristics may be too taxing and have the opposite, negative effect on motivation and engagement.

For example, among K-12 teachers, the pandemic increased the health risk of in-person teaching. To avoid this risk, many teachers were required to learn how to use internet platforms for distance teaching. For older employees, these new learning demands may reduce engagement and increase retirement intentions. On the other hand, job redesign to reduce physical demands and related health stresses may reduce retirement intentions among older employees but have no appreciable effect on work motivation among younger employees. Similarly, engagement may be positively or adversely affected by leadership and organizational politics, such as an inspirational CEO, or when the company is sold to another company.

Although work conditions can and do importantly affect motivation and engagement, managers often make the mistake of attributing an employee's motivation and job performance largely to the employee's personality (e.g., the employee is lazy or slow) without taking into account the employee's work experience (e.g., the task is repetitive, boring, or has become too demanding). Further, a large body of research shows that work motivation and engagement are not just a function of the employee's "personality" and work conditions, but also the employee's motives, beliefs, life goals, interests, and competencies – all of which change across the lifespan.[10]

A second way to enhance engagement and motivation is through joint goal setting and the provision of relevant, constructive feedback. Motivation is typically strongest when people adopt important, challenging, but realistic work goals *and* receive feedback indicating that they are making progress toward that goal. Explicit goal setting sessions with employees afford supervisors and employees an opportunity to align organizational and personal goals in ways that support employee motivation. Many leaders consider goal-setting sessions perfunctory and time-consuming. But these sessions allow for the development of a stronger employee-supervisor relationship and imbue an employee's daily work activities with greater meaning and value. Supervisors who want to improve employee motivation need to make the mental turn away from viewing goal setting meetings as procedural and impersonal. Instead, they should see these meetings as a chance to build a supportive relationship with the employee.

Goals can be assigned by the supervisor or set jointly by the supervisor and the employee. Participative goal setting provides an opportunity for building the supervisor-employee relationship and revising work goals in a way that can better utilize the employee's talents and skills. Studies show that participative goal setting yields higher employee motivation and performance than assigned goals.[11] For older workers who may be experiencing a change in resource availability (e.g., more care-giving responsibilities), participative goal setting is a particularly important format. For example, researchers have found the emergence of what is called generativity motives among people in their mid-to-late career. These motives refer to the desire to pass one's knowledge on to younger workers and to help younger employees become successful, for example though mentoring.[12] Among older workers with strong motives for teaching others (generativity), participative goal setting may yield work goals that include highly valued objectives by the employee.

Participative goal setting also allows the supervisor to convey performance expectations in a less threatening context, and to introduce tools and knowledge that can help the employee become a more valued performer. In a team situation, for example, goal setting discussions between the team leader and an older worker provide a format in which the leader can encourage the older worker to develop new skills and increase learning-oriented interactions with younger team members. Goal setting discussions are also important opportunities for supervisors to learn more about the older worker's broader plan for continued employment. For example, if a supervisor learns that an employee wants to retire within five years, work goals may be formulated in a way that facilitates the transition either to full retirement or a bridge retirement work role.

Work goals typically take time to accomplish. For most people, sustaining motivation and performance during goal striving requires feedback (also see Chapter 8 on feedback). Ironically, however, one of the most frequent complaints that employees have about their work situation is about the lack of feedback – namely, that supervisory feedback is too infrequent, comes too late, and is often only provided when the employee is not meeting goal expectations. Although employees typically receive feedback on immediate performance success and failure (e.g., from the machines they work with), it is feedback from supervisors and coworkers that activates the emotions and motives that most powerfully sustain work motivation. There are many ways that supervisors can make the most of giving feedback to employees. Special Focus Box 3.3 provides a list of feedback do's and don'ts with respect to enhancing motivation.

A third consideration is the match between what you want the employee to do and the incentive structure. In the early part of the 20th century (the industrial era), organizations often used piece-rate compensation plans to reward production speed on the assembly line. These reward systems had the effect of increasing employee production, but often at the cost of production quality. In the 21st century, routine assembly work is rapidly being taken over by robots, and human work has become more complex and less physically demanding. In today's jobs, high job performance requires the employee to be motivated toward problem-solving, creativity, and collaboration. Employee attributes such as arm strength are

Special Focus Box 3.3: Feedback Do's and Don'ts That Support Employee Motivation and Engagement

DO	DON'T
Provide **timely** feedback	Provide feedback many weeks or months later
Provide **constructive, respectful, and truthful** feedback (e.g., "Although you did not make your sales quota, I know you worked hard trying to meet your goal")	Don't provide feedback on the fly or in a way that does not allow the employee a way to see the path forward (e.g., "I need to see you about your screw-up")
Provide feedback **about the** *employee's behavior* – **not the employee as a person** (e.g., I was disappointed with the way the report was organized")	Don't provide judgmental feedback about the employee as a person (e.g., "due to your sloppiness")
Provide **formative** feedback as possible (e.g., "Have you talked to Hal about how to solve this kind of problem?"	Don't provide unexplained evaluative feedback (e.g., "You failed…"); instead provide specific feedback about what you expected
Provide feedback that fosters **employee trust**, not disbelief or suspicion	Don't blame other people for negative employee outcomes that are your decision
Provide **specific feedback** on what was right and what was wrong	Don't threaten or make fun of an employee to make a point about their performance – even in jest and never in public
Provide time to **allow the employee to respond** and discuss the feedback	Don't get off track. Provide feedback about the employee's progress toward meeting work goals; not feedback on unrelated personal matters (e.g., "I notice that you have lost a lot of weight")

less important today than psychological traits such as personal initiative, resourcefulness, and the ability to build strong interpersonal relations. The type of rewards you use will motivate employees to different kinds of performance.

In a sales office, for example, a compensation scheme based on number of sales made may result in more sales but not a higher sales total at the end of the quarter. If you want to see a higher sales total, then that is what you need to reward. If you want to motivate engagement, you need to provide opportunities and rewards for proactive behaviors, taking responsibility and helping other team members. In the 21st century, work motivation often means employees who are energized to take the initiative, to persist (within reason) despite fatigue and frustration, and to be a good organizational citizen and helpful team member. To build work motivation, rewards need to be provided for the behaviors and performance you want to encourage, not just the performance outcomes.

As we noted earlier, extrinsic rewards obviously remain important motivators. But the kind of behaviors that employers seek from their employees today often requires far more than just paying them well – they require that the job provide satisfaction of intrinsic motives common to all people – a sense of self-determination and belonging. Self-determination is enhanced by both managerial practices and job design. Jobs that provide a good fit between the employee's skills and work demands increase the opportunity for autonomy and higher levels of self-determination, that in turn is associated with job satisfaction, work engagement, and a lower likelihood of quitting.[13] Employees who believe that they can never meet their work goals or engage in work that does not allow them to use their skills may disengage from work to avoid feelings of incompetence or boredom, respectively. For example, a late-career employee who is never given the opportunity to use his accumulated skills or teach them to others may disengage from his work. Strong work motivation also requires the right kind of interpersonal environment – a social environment that supports a sense of belonging and being valued by others – regardless of one's background, age, or experience.

A final consideration relates to the beneficial effects that typically come with improving employee job attitudes and workplace emotions. Employees who maintain a positive attitude toward their work tend to view challenges more as opportunities rather than threats, and to take pride in their performance. In contrast, employees who experience low work motivation often report weaker positive attitudes toward their work. Such attitudes and negative feelings can, in turn, exacerbate feelings of job stress.

In summary, work motivation is not an attribute of the person or the situation alone. Rather, it emerges and evolves from the constant interaction that takes place between the employee and his/her social and physical environment. *Employees, managers, and organizations each play an important role in determining an individual's work motivation and engagement.* In the next sections, we will explore some of the critical employee characteristics and work environment forces that can affect motivation and engagement.

How People Differ: Compared to Each Other and Across the Lifespan

Most of us know that employees differ in what motivates them. Some employees are motivated by a promotion opportunity. Others are motivated by the opportunity to mentor others. But what contributes to these differences in motivation and engagement? Differences among people can be thought of in two ways: (1) how an employee differs compared to other people in general and (2) how employees change across the lifespan.

The first way that people differ – that is, differences *between* people are called *inter-individual* differences. These are the differences that we most commonly consider when making managerial judgments, such as who to promote. Some differences between people are obvious (e.g., height, ethnicity, gender); others, such as differences in personality, motives, goals, and interests, are less obvious. Personality traits influence how an individual interprets and responds to events and work situations. For example, anxious employees (employees higher in neuroticism compared to other employees) may interpret constructive supervisory feedback as criticism, and so become more anxious rather than more effective in their job. In contrast, employees low on this trait are more apt to interpret the same feedback as constructive, thus allowing them to focus greater attention to the task.

As managers, it is often easy to attribute an employee's motivation to personality trait differences. But in fact only two personality traits, conscientiousness and neuroticism, are significantly related to motivation.[14] Conscientiousness refers to the individual's tendency to be reliable and achievement oriented. People higher in Neuroticism tend to be more anxious, fearful, and more oriented toward threats than opportunities. So, while these traits can play a more direct role in job performance, other personality traits tend to come into play *only* in certain situations. For example, an individual who is very gregarious and extraverted may be more motivated in a job that requires high levels of social interaction than a job in which she works alone all day.

A second kind of difference that affects work motivation pertains to *intra-individual differences* – that is, the physical, cognitive, and emotional changes that *occur within a person* as a person ages. Until the mid-20th century, these differences and their effects on motivation were considered relatively unimportant since most people retired by age 65. Today, however, people often remain in the workforce well into their 70s. Intraindividual differences, or changes related to aging – also often form the basis for erroneous age-based stereotypes about older workers. As an example, age-based stereotypes of older workers as poorer performers continues to reverberate in managerial circles, although scientific and everyday evidence provides no support for this stereotype.[15]

We have previously discussed age-related changes in motivation and noted that aging does not reduce work motivation and engagement for everyone. We also note the evidence for how work motives change over the lifespan. So, how does aging affect and relate to work motivation and engagement? First, there are gradual declines in a number of important cognitive abilities, physical abilities, and psychomotor skills across the lifespan. With increasing age, people experience gradual declines in cognitive abilities related to memory and executive cognitive processes. When and how quickly these declines occur varies greatly from person to person, and how this affects motivation is not intuitive.

Researchers have identified two major types of cognitive abilities: (1) "fluid" intellectual abilities and (2) "crystallized" aspects of intelligence.[16] Fluid intellect includes abilities, such as short-term memory and processing speed, that decline with age. In contrast, crystallized intellect includes operations such as wisdom and job-related knowledge and skills that improve with age. Depending on job demands, crystallized knowledge may compensate for gradual age-related declines in fluid intellect until very late in adulthood. For example, Ruth Bader Ginsberg performed her job as Supreme Court judge well into her 80s. From a performance perspective, slight declines in fluid intelligence among older employees may be well compensated for by an employee's extensive job knowledge and experience. In jobs that place a premium on problem-solving, for example, older employees may be one of the most valuable members of a work team, as was shown by pilot Chelsey Sullenberger's success at age 57 in guiding an emergency plane landing on the Hudson river. However, in jobs that make heavy demands on age-sensitive psychomotor or physical skills, like race car driving or delivery drivers, older adults may have a more difficult time maintaining high performance despite high motiv-ation. As these examples illustrate, the impact of age-related changes on work motivation and performance critically depends on the employee's ability to meet the demands of the job.

Second, there are also age-related differences in personality traits and attitudes. Personality research findings show that in the United States, neuroticism and extraversion decline across the lifespan while agreeableness and conscientiousness increase.[17] These findings provide support for the popular belief that, all other things equal, older employees may be more reliable than younger employees. Again, however, using age stereotypes may result in misjudgments. Employees vary compared to each other – for example, some people are always more reliable than others, regardless of age. Unreliability at work is more likely a reflection of how the employee functions (and has always functioned) compared to others, rather than a function of age-related changes in personality, or the fact that they are a "lazy Millennial". Using age stereotypes or age-related personality generalizations to judge or evaluate an individual's behavior or motivation is a notoriously bad shorthand for understanding what drives employees. A far better strategy is to learn how the job may exceed the employee's constraints and what drives or spurs the employee.

A third way that individuals change as they age pertains to how they envision their work future. How people anticipate their occupational future can importantly affect work motivation.[18] Early in adulthood most people envision a work future that is long-lived and filled with opportunities and few constraints. As people age and experience age-related changes in different abilities, they envision a future with fewer opportunities for development and more constraints. Depending on organizational and broader socio-cultural norms, they may also begin to think of their work future as part-time or retired workers. However, occupational future time perspective and work motivation may be increased among mid- to late-career employees by providing supportive supervision for new skill learning and opportunities for job crafting to better match their changing skills.

Motivating a Longer Working Life

Most managers focus on motivating employees *at* work. However, as the workforce ages in many developed countries, policy makers and organizational personnel have focused on developing programs that promote healthy, high-performing late-career workers who want to continue working past traditional retirement age (i.e., motivation *to* work).[19] Motivating employees to continue working later in life requires work role redesign and human resource management practices that accommodate older worker constraints and satisfy older worker goals and motives.

Work Role Redesign

Over the past two decades, organizations have allowed more and more high-performing older workers to collaborate with their supervisor to redesign their work role as a means of motivating continued employment past traditional retirement age. For example, older employees who have performed the same tasks for decades may feel that their work has become boring and offer little in the way of challenge. Work role redesign may be used to increase task variety and/or provide time and support for learning new skills. Work role redesign can also be used to mitigate growing person-job misfit due to age-related changes in employee abilities. In this case, the work role may be reconfigured to avoid tasks that make strong demands on physical or cognitive abilities and more intensely utilize the employee's durable and often unique job skills. Commercial pilots, for example, are currently required to retire from flying at age 65 regardless of health. However, airlines may reassign them to support positions such as simulation instructor. Similarly, utility line workers who are unable to meet the physical demands of a field line job may modify their work role to make greater use of their job-related knowledge by training new workers or serving as consultants on special projects.

Implementing New HR Practices

Older workers often experience increased nonwork demands, such as spousal caregiving. Rather than forcing these workers to choose between continued employment and satisfying nonwork demands, a growing number of organizations have instituted human resource management practices that offer employees greater flexibility in scheduling work hours, working from home, and self-managing vacation and sick days.[20] Snowbird programs represent one type of HR practice aimed at retaining older workers. Organizations, such as Home Depot and CVS, offer snowbird programs that allow older employees to work in different parts of the country part of the year. Other organizations have encouraged motivation by removing obstacles to employment related to transportation (e.g., providing free shuttle service to the parking lot for employees working at night). Still, other organizations have developed employee recognition programs aimed at older employees, or have offered free classes and coaching in planning for life goals, such as financial security in retirement and achieving a healthy lifestyle. (See Chapter 7 for more information on how to help employees improve work-family balance.)

Enhancing Work Motivation Regardless of Age

The previous section focused on motivating mid-to-late-career employees. Regardless of age, however, work motivation and engagement are optimized for most people under four conditions. First, work motivation is higher when the work role promotes a positive professional identity, a sense of belonging, a sense of competence, and feelings of job satisfaction. The pride of a job well done and recognized by others is a deeply rewarding experience for most employees. Intrinsic work motivation for all employees is promoted when the work role is aligned with an employee's capabilities and resources (e.g., a job in which the worker is neither bored nor stressed by the work pace and activities). When there is a good fit, it is also usually easier to afford the employee some freedom and control over their daily activities and task strategies (e.g., organizing one's own daily task schedule).

Second, in this age of audacious goals, like going to Mars, developing a vaccine for COVID-19, and building electric vehicles, a growing number of people work in teams. Meaningful team and organization goals provide most employees with a sense of greater purpose for their work than single acts (e.g., an Amazon warehouse worker who is helping people at risk get the goods they need; a fire fighter building a break line to protect people's homes). Reminding people of the meaning their work has for society and others can also support work motivation when setbacks occur.

At the same time, motivation is also strongly influenced by daily experiences. Having a boss who micromanages or treats an employee differently than others can reduce work motivation and create stress no matter how noble the team's goal. The third condition for optimizing work motivation and engagement is to create a work culture and explicit behavioral norms that promote and enforce fairness and cooperation. Obviously not all employees will like or want to work with one another. But keeping the focus on work tasks and team goals, treating people respectfully, and evaluating subordinates on the basis of their performance rather than your preferences, are powerful ways to promote such a culture.

The fourth condition for optimizing work motivation pertains to understanding the role of aging in work motivation. Differences in work motivation and engagement occur across the lifespan and life course. Aging influences the ease of new skill learning and physical competencies, work-life balance, and the work goals that are most important to employees. Younger workers with a growing family and strong interest in occupational advancement may find repetitive jobs lack challenge and opportunity. On the other hand, mid-to-late-career employees with caregiving demands may be more interested in job security and opportunities to use existing skills rather than opportunities for career advancement.

Obviously, it is not always possible for managers or organizational leaders to create environments that optimize work motivation and engagement for all employees. However, empowering and listening to your subordinates can increase the likelihood that you can come up with resourceful and creative solutions to engaging your workforce more of the time.

Summary

Managers often relate that employee motivation and engagement is the "secret sauce" for a successful team and organization. Building on research findings accumulated over the past century, we describe the basic ingredients of this secret sauce and how motivation changes as a function of the employee, the work role, and the workplace, with special attention to mid- and late-career employees. We repeatedly stress that successful development of an engaged workforce does not happen overnight and rarely by accident. People management is a continuous process; there is no single best practice that can be used with all people all the time. Extrinsic incentives, such as extra pay, often have an initial positive effect but should be used sparingly since their effect wears off quickly and these incentives can dampen intrinsic motivation. To be sure, extrinsic incentives do matter; they remain powerful influences on the decision to take a job or to continue working past normal retirement age. But once on the job, employee engagement and effort may be driven by different factors, including age-related differences in work goals. Modern approaches to employee motivation and engagement focus on providing work roles and environments that address intrinsic motives and provide a sense of purpose or meaningfulness.

Think of employee motivation and engagement as a three-legged stool. Employee needs and motives represent one leg of the stool. The job and work role represent the second leg of the stool. And the culture and norms of the workplace represent the third leg of the stool. To maintain motivation and engagement, organizations and supervisors must evaluate whether adjustments are needed *any time there is a change in any leg of the stool.* In today's work world, the stool's balance can be upset by changes in any of the three legs of the stool. Population trends have increased age-diversity at work and led to a greater array of employee needs and motives. At the same time, automation has brought about changes that has changed many work roles and often requires new skill learning. And new organizational leadership and broader societal and natural forces (e.g., pandemics, disasters) have brought about changes in the work environment that disrupt engrained work routines.

This volume details the multiple strategies available for building and sustaining employee motivation as a consequence of these dynamic changes. Sometimes, employee motivation can be enhanced by changing the employee's work role (see Chapter 4 on skills updating and job crafting); other times engagement can be improved by changing the socio-emotional context in which work takes place (see Chapter 8 on strategies to encourage employee growth). And yet at other times, employee motivation may be increased by providing a workplace that accommodates age-related changes in abilities (see Chapter 5). Through these strategies, organizational leaders can play a critical role in making work more motivating and personally rewarding. For example, managers can enhance motivation in even the most repetitive of jobs, such as assembly line manufacturing of medical masks, by connecting the employees' activities to the product's consumers (e.g., healthcare workers). Contrary to popular belief, strategies to enhance work motivation often occur as part of normal supervision, rather than as a special initiative. Whether you are a leader, manager, or front-line supervisor, employee motivation and engagement matter to your bottom line.

PIERA Example: Sustaining Work Motivation in the Midst of Technological Change: A Case Study

Our demonstration of the PIERA method in this chapter presents a case example, where PIERA was applied to identifying and addressing a work motivation problem in a valued employee. Think about what you would have done at each step along the way and whether any of these ideas can be adapted to your own organization.

Background

Aaron was a midcareer line worker in a large carpet manufacturing plant. Plant employees work in small teams that cover different portions of the production process. Aaron and his team work in the fiber production area. After years on the job, Aaron has learned about how the machines in his section work and how to fix any one of them when a problem arises. Because fiber production involves multiple steps, Aaron often visits with team members in adjoining areas to let them know about problems, delays, and other issues in his area that will affect production in their area. Aaron's job also demands miles of daily walking between machines every shift, and regular meetings between his team with their supervisor to identify new production goals and upcoming changes to the line.

Aaron has worked for the company 18 years and has developed strong friendships with other team members, many of whom are similar in age. During the past few years, the company has updated the manufacturing process, resulting in continuous changes in Aaron's work role. Most of these changes have reduced Aaron's autonomy and his sense of contribution to the process. New machines have been installed that self-correct relatively simple problems, and provide operators with feedback at a central work station, reducing how much Aaron walks each day. Having to spend more time at his station has decreased the number of daily opportunities Aaron gets to socialize with other team members on the floor. Aaron's supervisor, Mary, noted that Aaron was acting less engaged and that he was not regularly communicating production issues downstream to other teams. She chatted with him briefly about these missed opportunities, but Aaron was defensive and denied he was dissatisfied with his job.

Planning

This is the first step in a PIERA approach. Planning a motivational intervention actually occurs in two stages. First, although Aaron's behavior change appears a function of motivation, you need to make sure that what you are observing is indeed due to a change in engagement and motivation, and not to equipment or lack of training. In Aaron's case, his lack of attention to communicating with other team members does indeed appear to be motivational rather than due to equipment or know-how. The changes in the plant have reduced Aaron's freedom of movement, job scope, relevance in keeping production machines working, and socializing opportunities. After considering the impact of these changes from Aaron's point-of-view, Mary reasons that the consequence has been to lessen Aaron's job involvement and motivation for activities that promote higher levels of overall production.

Once Mary decided that the problem was motivational, she proceeded to the second planning stage. At this point, she considered whether an intervention was worth her time and effort. Aaron knows the production process very well and is a valued team member. His declining motivation suggested to Mary that he might quit his job when another attractive opportunity came his way. Thinking through what would change if the intervention was successful, Mary decided to focus on one measurable objective; namely, an increase in the number of times that Aaron alerts other teams about upcoming slowdowns or issues in his section that will affect them.

The next step in Mary's plan was to develop and test-drive her strategy. Which interventions are possible? Since she did not have control over compensation, she could not use an extrinsic reward. That leaves interventions that leverage her ability to provide information and support to Aaron that, in turn, increase his feelings of competence and value to the organization. Mary also needed to figure out how to measure the effects of the intervention on Aaron's behavior. Which units and leaders could she count on for support in this area? How long should the intervention last and how would she celebrate his goal success? Finally, and possibly most importantly, how would she get Aaron's buy-in for this intervention? In developing her plan, Mary consulted often with her peers to get ideas that help refined the plan.

Implementation

Wanting to enhance employee motivation and doing so are two separate things. Mary's plan required patience, time, and attention. To get Aaron's buy-in, she decided to present the plan in a way that allowed Aaron to contribute and feel valued. She introduced the intervention as a way of enhancing plant performance. Mary suggested that she wanted to conduct an "experiment" to see how the frequency of Aaron's interteam communications affected downstream performance. She encouraged Aaron to participate in setting a realistic, but challenging weekly performance goal, and to discussing and together resolving potential drawbacks to the "experiment". Mary had also planned ahead for how to introduce the method of performance measurement, and ways to ensure that Aaron would feel treated respectfully and fairly. Aaron agreed to try it out. Once the intervention was underway, she checked with Aaron on how things were going. She recorded performance weekly and took regular notes on the nature of the Aaron's communications and his reactions to the intervention.

Evaluation

After 3 weeks (15 work days), Mary reviewed her notes, Aaron's performance, and the production performance data. Although Aaron had increased the frequency of his downstream team communications (the goal of the intervention), there was no appreciable effect on production efficiency. It was also unclear that Aaron's work engagement has changed much, other than his higher rate of communication to the downstream team.

Reflection

At this point, Mary considered a number of different explanations. Her intention had been to increase Aaron's engagement, and although she was successful in changing one aspect of his work behavior, she did not see any appreciable change in his overall work motivation or engagement. She reconsidered what factors might have accounted for his declining work motivation in the first place. Had it been the reduced role he played in fixing the machines? Was it the reduced autonomy he experienced as a result of having a workstation? She recalled that there had been several new hires lately; people much younger than Aaron who seemed to work more easily than Aaron with the new technologies.

Adjustment

Mary called Aaron in to discuss the results. She thanked him for the increase in downstream communications and asked him how he felt about the intervention. Gradually, she moved the conversation toward his work goals and how she might be able to help him accomplish those goals. It had been over a decade since a supervisor had asked him about his work goals, and Aaron felt valued by the supervisor. He indicated that he had become bored with his current job and was looking for a way to learn skills related to running the new machines and to advancing to a more responsible, supervisory position. She told him she appreciated his candor and set up another meeting to discuss possibilities.

At the next meeting, she asked Aaron if he would be willing to spend time in a dual mentoring relationship with a new, younger employee. Aaron would mentor the new employee in exchange for the younger employee teaching Aaron about the technology driving the new machines. Mary also asked whether

Aaron would be willing to lead a small group of employees representing different sections of the plant in a taskforce aimed at improving plant safety. Although there would be no paid compensation for this role, the supervisor offered flexibility in his scheduled hours during the length of the taskforce project. Aaron seemed pleased with the change in responsibilities and looked forward to mentoring new employees.

QUESTIONS TO PONDER:

Was Aaron's engagement problem "fixed?" Why or why not?

What other things could Mary have done to engage Aaron in his changing work role?

Are there lessons from this PIERA example that could be adapted to your work environment?

Action Items: Things to Do Right Now, Next Week, Long Term

Right Now

If you haven't already, take a few minutes to look over Special Focus Box 3.2 about your motivational style. What are your initial ideas about your style as you reflect on these questions? Take a few notes as a place to start.

Next Week

Over the next week, pay attention to how you interact with the members of your team. Do you observe yourself acting in accordance with the style you thought you had? Have you surprised yourself in any way? Also, think about whether you find yourself using different strategies with people depending on their age. Why do you think you do that?

Long Term

Think about which motivational strategies you would like to try with members of your team that you hadn't tried before. How can PIERA guide you in testing out some new interventions? Take a look at your calendar and the expected cadence of business over the next several months. Is there a good time to try a new strategy? Thinking about when you'd ultimately like to see a change, work backward, and start planning for the stages of PIERA. Who else should you get on board?

Notes

1. Kanfer, R. (2012). Work motivation: Theory, practice, and future directions. In S. W. Kozlowski (Ed.), *The Oxford handbook of industrial and organizational psychology* (pp. 455–495). Oxford, UK: Blackwell. Also see Pinder, C. S. (2008). *Work motivation in organizational behavior.* UK: Psychology Press.
2. Berg, J. M., Dutton, J. E., & Wrzesniewski, A. (2013). Job crafting and meaningful work. In B. J. Dik, Z. S. Byrne, & M. F. Steger (Eds.), *Purpose and meaning in the workplace* (pp. 81–104). New York: American Psychological Association.
3. Deci, E. L., Koestner, R., & Ryan, R. M. (1999). A meta-analytic review of experiments examining the effects of extrinsic rewards on intrinsic motivation. *Psychological Bulletin, 125*(3), 627–668.
4. Deci, E. L., Connell, J. P., & Ryan, R. M. (1989). Self-determination in a work organization. *Journal of Applied Psychology, 74,* 580–590.
5. Inceoglu, I., Segers, J., & Bartram, D. (2012). Age-related differences in work motivation. *Journal of Occupational and Organizational Psychology, 85,* 300–329.
6. Kooij, D., de Lange, A., Jansen, P., Kanfer, R., & Dikkers, J. (2011). Age and work related motives: Results of a meta-analysis. *Journal of Organizational Behavior, 32,* 197–225.
7. Knight, C., Patterson, M., & Dawson, J. (2017). Building work engagement: A systematic review and meta-analysis investigating the effectiveness of work engagement interventions. *Journal of Organizational Behavior, 38,* 792–812.
8. Ibid.
9. Dalal, R. S., Bhave, D. P., & Fiset, J. (2014). Within-person variability in job performance. *Journal of Management, 40,* 1396–1436.
10. Finkelstein, L., Truxillo, D., Fraccaroli, F., & Kanfer, R. (Eds.). (2015). *Facing the challenges of a multi-age workforce: A use-inspired approach.* New York: Psychology Press.
11. Latham, G. P., & Yukl, G. A. (1975). Assigned versus participative goal setting with educated and uneducated woods workers. *Journal of Applied Psychology, 60,* 299–302.
12. Peterson, B. E., & Stewart, A. J. (1996). Antecedents and contexts of generativity motivation at midlife. *Psychology and Aging, 11,* 21–33.
13. Kristof-Brown, A. L., Zimmerman, R. D., & Johnson, E. C. (2005). Consequences of individuals' fit at work: A meta-analysis of person-job, person-organization, person-group, and person-supervisor fit. *Personnel Psychology, 58,* 281–342.

14. Judge, T. A., & Ilies, R. (2002). Relationship of personality to performance motivation: A meta-analytic review. *Journal of Applied Psychology, 87*(4), 797–807.

15. Ng, T. W. H., & Feldman, D. C. (2008). The relationship of age to ten dimensions of job performance. *Journal of Applied Psychology, 93*(2), 392–423.

16. Cattell, R. B. (1987). *Intelligence: Its structure, growth, and action.* Elsevier Science Publishers. Also see Ackerman, P. L. (1996). A theory of adult intellectual development: Process, personality, interests, and knowledge. *Intelligence, 22*(2), 227–257.

17. Chopik, W. J., & Kitayama, S. (2018). Personality change across the lifespan: Insights from a cross-cultural longitudinal study. *Journal of Personality, 86,* 508–521.

18. Zacher, H., & Frese, M. (2009). Remaining time and opportunities at work: Relationships between age, work characteristics, and occupational future time perspective. *Psychology and Aging, 24,* 487.

19. Kanfer, R., Beier, M. E., & Ackerman, P. L. (2012). Goals and motivation related to work in later adulthood: An organizing framework. *European Journal of Work and Organizational Psychology,* 1–12.

20. The age premium: Retaining older workers. *The New York Times,* May 15, 2014.

Training and Learning as Workers Evolve in a Technology-Driven World

4

As we have stated throughout this book, the workforce is aging and becoming more age-diverse, with people of different ages working together. But there is also an economic and societal backdrop to this change which is making this situation yet more complex. First, jobs are changing rapidly, meaning that workers will need to adapt their skills to changing job requirements. This may be due to the introduction of new technology into the job, or it may be a result of jobs changing as workplace configurations change – or due to societal changes and events. A recent example would be new "work from home" configurations for many workers due to COVID-19. A similar example closer to home for the authors of this book is delivering university courses online – quite a shift after a career of classroom teaching. Our point is that, over their careers, employees may be expected to learn new skills, even if they stay in the same field of work, and even with the same job title.

Second, some jobs are being eliminated completely, due to automation or the use of artificial intelligence. The implications of this phenomenon are that many workers will need to learn new skills in order to remain in the workforce, and many of these workers may have to take on these development activities later in their careers.

Third, many training methods are delivered using new methods of training delivery such as mobile devices. While these may not be difficult training methods to master in themselves – many of the newest training methods were developed with ease of use in mind – they may be intimidating to learners who have never used these training platforms before. While studies have shown that older and younger employees are comparable in their comfort with technology, we point out that the workplace is requiring upskilling from all employees regarding the use of new technology. The implication of this economic and social backdrop is that most people will need to continue to develop their work skills across their working lives. The notion of "lifelong learning" probably has differential attractiveness for younger and older workers. For older employees, the introduction of new technologies that disrupt routines honed over decades may be resisted, regardless of how easy the technology is to learn or use. For example, among older mechanics who have developed advanced diagnostic trouble-shooting skills, new technologies that automate this activity may lessen a sense of expertise more than they would for younger workers who have not had time to develop expertise in this area.

Although learning new work skills can be challenging for workers of any age, it presents different sets of issues for workers of different ages. First, while it is untrue that older workers are not able or willing to learn, they may have different training needs and motivations than their younger counterparts. In addition, people's self-confidence (aka "self-efficacy") about their ability to learn may vary at different ages, a factor that can affect their learning. And if the need to learn new skills comes in the context of job loss, this reduction in self-confidence can be exacerbated. Finally, as we discuss in Chapter 4, with aging comes some cognitive changes. However, most of these are subtle and they vary considerably across individuals. Most important, there are many ways in which age-related cognitive changes can be addressed.

In this chapter, we'll examine training, learning, and development within the context of aging. Our goal is to give you a better understanding of how age may affect job-related learning. By better understanding these issues, you should be better able to apply the PIERA framework to developing an effective approach to training and development for late-career workers – all the while ensuring that the training addresses the needs of workers at different career stages. We'll begin by providing an overview of the science on workplace learning and then discuss age differences that may affect training at work. From there we will summarize some of the steps that can be taken to address age-related issues and learning, concluding with a discussion of how to apply the PIERA approach to training.

Training and Development: Science and Best Practices

Before we discuss how to develop an age-sensitive training system, it's helpful to briefly describe the science behind training and development. Many best practices for organizational training programs have developed over the last 30 years, and there is a significant body of research on how to make workplace training most effective. In addition, these practices are relevant whether choosing a fairly modest bit of training or designing a more ambitious organization-wide training program.[1]

Training Needs Assessment

What is it that employees need to learn? One of the most important ways to ensure the quality of a training program is to include a training needs assessment (TNA). In PIERA terms, TNA is part of planning. It assures that before a training program is developed or implemented that it's the *right* program for the situation. Briefly, effective TNA includes (see Figure 4.1):

- Determining the characteristics and needs of the *organization*, such as its and culture, which jobs need training attention, and the resources that it can devote to training. This information can be gathered through surveys or discussions with management and employees.
- Determining the tasks and responsibilities that make up the *jobs* that need training, and the knowledge and skills a person needs to perform those jobs. This might be uncovered through reviewing job descriptions, job analyses and competency models (if available), speaking with workers and their supervisors, and surveys.
- Assessing current *skills gaps of employees* in those jobs. These skills gaps will guide what is to be trained. These skills gaps might be identified by reviewing employee or organizational performance records, speaking with employees or supervisors, and by surveys.
- Determining the key *employee characteristics* that should be kept in mind when developing the training, such as their age, education, and attitudes about training.

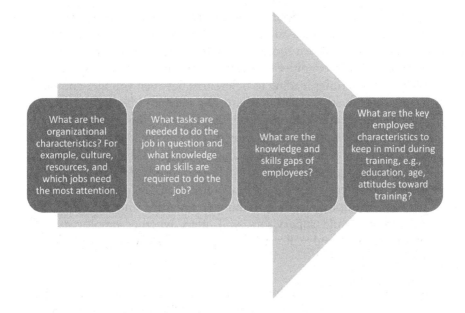

Figure 4.1   Steps in a training needs assessment

Trainee Characteristics and Contextual Issues

Because training helps people to learn, it is very important to take into account the different knowledge, skills, and motives of the employees who will be taking training. The better the program can adapt to trainee characteristics, the more effective it can be. For example:

- *Trainee self-efficacy.* Employees differ in their confidence for new skill learning, and that confidence can affect their learning motivation and success. When employees have low self-efficacy, it is important that the training program be set up in such a way as to help employees develop a "can do" mindset to learning and set up training in ways that maximize the employee's control over their learning process.
- Research shows that during learning, all people engage in activities that allow them to assess their skills, their learning progress, and the amount of attention and effort required to advance. These activities are typically referred to as *meta-cognition,* and people differ in terms of their *meta-cognitive skills*. Meta-cognitive skills affect how well people learn by directing their attention and effort during the learning process.

- People differ in their *cognitive abilities* in two ways. First, people differ within a group of their similar-aged peers. People with higher cognitive abilities may learn more quickly than those with lower cognitive abilities. Second, cognitive abilities change in predictable ways over the lifespan, sometimes leading to differences between younger and older trainees. However, whether there are reliable differences between different age groups critically depends on the way the training program is structured. For example, training that places high demands on short-term memory tends to favor younger employees, but programs that rely on background knowledge can favor older employees.
- People don't learn new job skills in a vacuum. The *organizational context*, for example, whether training is rewarded and valued by top management and supervisors, will affect whether employees care about learning and will actually apply their knowledge ("transfer") back into the job.

Taken together, these individual differences and context differences affect employee *motivation to learn* – the effort they will put into learning – a key determinant of training success. (We say more about motivation in general in Chapter 3.) Motivation to learn is also affected by factors such as whether training goals are clearly stated and whether it is clear to employees that there is "something in it for them". These factors can also affect *motivation to participate in training,* or willingness to participate in a particular training program at hand. Motivation to learn and motivation to participate in training are both partly driven by whether the training seems relevant to the job.

Choosing Training Methods

Choosing the method of training is similar to identifying the strategy component of planning in the PIERA model. The choice of a strategy depends on many things, including the training needs assessment, the organizational context, and what resources the organization has available for training. Any number of training strategies may be used and/or combined, including for example, on-the-job training, lectures, technology-mediated training (such as using high-fidelity simulators for training); or having trainees observe (model) the behavior they are to learn, such as how to operate some type of software or to counsel a difficult employee. Each method has advantages and disadvantages; we'll discuss these in the context of late-career workers later in the chapter.

Evaluation of the Training

This step of training is consistent with the evaluation component of the PIERA model. Most organizations today expect that some form of evaluation be conducted following a training so that organizations can reflect on whether the time, money, and effort spent on the training has impacted employee attitudes, knowledge, skills, and on-the-job performance. We discuss these in greater detail in Special Focus Box 4.1.

Special Focus Box 4.1: The Four Levels of Training Outcomes

The classic four "levels" of training outcomes, from most simple to most complex and rigorous, were developed over 60 years ago by Donald Kirkpatrick. Although there are now other approaches to thinking about training evaluation, the simplicity of Kirkpatrick's approach is part of its popularity. Here's a summary of Kirkpatrick's approach:

- At the most basic level, trainee **reactions** are how trainees react to the training. This might include asking trainees whether they enjoyed the training or whether they found the training to be useful. This might be assessed through a survey or by speaking with the employees during or after the training.
- **Learning** is whether any learning took place as a result of training, perhaps by giving a test or other assessment at the end of training.
- Even more ambitious and useful are training evaluations which allow for assessing whether training improved **behavior** back on the job (aka learning transfer). Although changes in job behavior are one of the main goals of training, it can be hard to determine if training caused behavior change because so many other factors besides training can affect the transfer of learned skills. This might be assessed with performance ratings or units produced.
- And finally, **results** is whether the training led to key organizational outcomes, such as increased profits or a decrease in medical errors. Of course, results outcomes are especially challenging because outcomes like profit can be affected by many things besides training.

Kirkpatrick, D. L. (1998). Evaluating training programs: The four levels (2nd ed.). San Francisco, CA: Berrett-Koehler.

Different evaluation methods should reflect what the training is supposed to change. For example, if the focus of training is on helping employees develop less ageist attitudes toward co-workers, questions to assess potential attitude change after training may be sufficient. As the evaluation process becomes more complex, however, it may be more difficult to determine whether training or some other factor (e.g., economic conditions) affected the outcome. Regardless, evaluation data are most useful in helping to decide whether to keep the training program as-is or whether it needs adjustment. Finally, it can be extremely useful to understand the effects of the training process itself: how trainees and trainers viewed the experience. This might take the form of talking with trainees and trainers during the implementation of the training program about what they think is going well or poorly during so that adjustments can be made mid-course.

Conclusion

While a full discussion of training best practices is beyond the scope of this book, we point out these specific issues because they are all relevant to training that addresses age and career-stage differences among learners. We also highlight two points. First, understanding the science behind organizational training, and the factors that lead to its success (or failure), will help you approach the issue of developing an effective, age-sensitive training and development plan for your organization. The best practices described identify the key "levers" that can be used to enhance training success. Second, best practices for employee training share many characteristics of the PIERA approach. Both take into account an initial assessment of organizational needs, the needs and characteristics of the employees, and the organizational context. Moreover, both approaches emphasize an evaluation of whether or not the program is working so that it can be adjusted.

How Might Age Differences Play a Role in Training?

While we know that there are several differences that come with age, most of them are not particularly relevant to a person's ability to learn. Here we describe two that may be – cognitive changes and concepts related to motivation to learn – examining how much and when they might affect the training of older workers.

Cognitive Skills

Given the importance of cognitive skills to learning, let's touch on how cognitive changes may affect learning. We cover the topic of cognitive skills only briefly here as this is covered in greater detail in Chapters 3 and 5.

First, we know that there may be some decline in what is called "fluid" intelligence over the lifespan, starting in a person's early 20s. Fluid intelligence involves working memory and the speed at which we process information. However, we also know that these changes are usually very gradual and may be compensated for by increases in "crystallized" intelligence, or the knowledge we accumulate about the world and our job. Because most jobs involve a mix of tasks that demand fluid intelligence and crystallized knowledge, gradual declines in fluid intelligence typically matter most to learning and new skill acquisition, rather than routinized and habitual job tasks. In the context of learning new skills, simple accommodations such as providing older learners with more time or control over the pace of learning are often helpful. Perhaps what's most important to keep in mind, however, is that decline in cognitive skills later in life varies considerably from person to person. Some people may experience notable decline while other people experience very little through most of later life.

Motivation to Learn May Sometimes Go Down a Little with Age – But It Depends

One common stereotype of older workers is that they don't want to learn new things. But is this stereotype of older employees even true? (Technically, a stereotype is a generalization that all people in a particular group – like all older workers – hold a specific characteristic. If we think of it that way, it would be impossible for that to be true!) One point we have made throughout this book is that most of the stereotypes about older workers are not true. However, to examine this issue empirically, one research team did a meta-analysis – a large summary of the available research – to examine the accuracy of six common stereotypes of older workers. Thomas Ng and Daniel Feldman[2] analyzed 418 studies that included over 200,000 people to examine six common age stereotypes, specifically, whether older workers are:

- less motivated at work
- more resistant to change
- less trusting
- less healthy
- more likely to have work-life imbalance issues, and
- less willing to participate in career development and training.

Ng and Feldman found that **none** of these stereotypes were true – although the last one may be more common for older workers in some occupations. Indeed, older workers may be less willing than younger workers to take on new training or career development – although the differences were fairly small. Specifically, the study found that older workers may have slightly lower career development motivation and motivation to learn. Why might this be?

Consider the example of an older worker, Javier, who is 64 and the manager of a product distribution warehouse for a medical supply company. Javier's job includes managing the distribution of products to retailers and medical centers around the country, as well as monitoring and managing product shipments from various manufacturers around the country and the world into the warehouse. As a leader, Javier is well respected by his team, and his manager and coworkers see him as a font of organizational knowledge for the company and its procedures. He is also well known for training and advising junior workers on his team. Javier enjoys his work, and while he could afford to retire now, he had planned to hold out until his full retirement age of 67. However, because the company has recently merged with another medical supply company, the software system used to manage the flow of products into and out of the warehouse will be changing so that the entire, merged organization can use the same system. Javier is frustrated by this decision, since it means that he will have to learn an entirely new software system. He knows the old system so well and is so close to retirement. In fact, he's frustrated enough that he has spoken with his boss about taking retirement sooner than planned; he argues that staying would require that he be trained on a skill that he will only need for a few years. Javier's boss has asked him to reconsider an early retirement because of his value to the team. But his boss has also made it clear that the new software will be coming in and that everyone will need to be trained on the new system, especially Javier because of his role.

We use the example of Javier to illustrate why some older workers may not be motivated to go through training and how this can be quite logical, sometimes even adaptive for them personally. Why invest in a new skill that will only be used for a short time? Research suggests that younger workers, most of whom have not yet acquired the job skills they need, will be focused on acquiring those job skills. By the same token, many older workers may prefer – and find it more satisfying and useful – to focus on applying the skills that they have accumulated, rather than acquiring lots of new skills. Indeed, this is consistent with research showing that younger people are more motivated and more satisfied by extrinsic aspects of the job – things like advancement, pay, and skill acquisition. In contrast, older workers will be more satisfied by intrinsic factors (e.g., the pleasure of doing the job itself) and by the interpersonal aspects of the work.[3] From this standpoint, Javier's reluctance to acquire new skills (as opposed to applying his considerable existing skills) makes sense. Also, just because Javier isn't interested in new training on this software doesn't mean that he isn't interested in learning more generally.

In fact, in their meta-analysis, Ng and Feldman cite a number of reasons that some older workers (again, not *all* by any means) may have lower training motivation – and ways to address these. One possibility is the decline in some cognitive skills that may slow the speed at which a person learns. Although this doesn't seem to be the case for Javier, if it were this might be addressed by providing him with support to learn at his own speed or using a flexible training system that allows people, regardless of their age, to move through the training at their own pace. (This is in fact an important characteristic of many online training systems.)

Second, as Javier's case suggests, it is common for midlife and older people to be aware of how much time they have remaining at work. As perceived time left in the workplace decreases, older workers might not want to invest in skills they won't need for very long. One solution might be for Javier's manager to see if the introduction of the new system can be postponed a bit, or barring that, what incentives she might give to Javier (an assistant? training support? a new role where he can use his existing skills to the company's advantage?) so as to retain this valuable employee. Also, given that research also shows that older workers value investing in personal relationships, Javier might be charged with helping his team to work through the training process for the new software. In this way, the cost of new skill learning for Javier can be offset by the potential rewards associated with helping his team develop new skills.

A third but all-too-common source of demotivation among late-career employees stems from organizational actions that suggest age bias. For example, this might happen when an employee perceives that the organization is more likely to offer training to younger than older workers. This could even lead older employees to be more apprehensive of doing poorly if they are offered training opportunities. This is clearly a sign of larger problems in the organization regarding making resources available to people of all ages – and unfortunate given the compelling research that shows that making resources available to workers of all ages has a definite upside. A large study of 93 German firms found that fair HR practices for people regardless of age – including equal access to training – benefited workers of *all* ages, young and old, creating a positive age climate and leading to increased company performance and decreased intentions to quit.[4]

Differences in Self-Efficacy and Meta-Cognitive Skills May also Play a Role

Another motivation-related issue that Ng and Feldman found in their meta-analysis – and one that is especially important to the issue of training – is that older workers seemed to have slightly lower learning self-efficacy compared to younger workers. As we mentioned earlier, self-efficacy (self-confidence) is essential to learning, and thus organizations should examine ways to address this age-related difference. This might follow the same suggestions we just made – provide training that is flexible and takes into account differences among learners, allowing people to go at their own speed and providing support to learners of all ages. Similarly, it has been noted that some older workers may have lower meta-cognitive skills, that is, be less able to assess their own abilities and thus direct their efforts to where they need training. Therefore, training methods that provide this guidance to learners may be most helpful.[5] Finally, keep in mind that making age overly salient to learners, such as by pointing out age as an issue in learning, or suggesting that older members may need special help, can definitely dampen learning. That is, making an "older learner" stereotype salient is not helpful.

It is important to make a few final points with regard to training motivation and the late-career worker. We want to re-emphasize the finding that chronological age is only weakly related to learning motivation. Most older workers do not lose interest in learning new skills, and that there is a lot of variability among older workers in this regard.

Indeed, many older workers want to learn new job skills, either because they enjoy their work, feel that new skills will keep them employable, or simply like learning new things. It should also be noted that late-career workers can provide considerable value in terms of training or mentoring junior colleagues. Their accumulated skills can make them a great resource, especially if they are provided with the right supports to help them become good trainers and mentors. And in addition to their increased focus on meaningful work and relationships at work, many older workers also develop generativity motives, that is, a desire to give back to the next generation. In fact, training and mentoring roles may be attractive to many older workers, many of whom are motived by doing meaningful work, interacting with others, and applying their accumulated job skills, leading to increased engagement in their work.[6] At the same time that older workers can share their knowledge with younger workers, younger workers can offer older workers assistance in developing new technical skills. Such "reverse mentoring" practices have the potential for developing new skills among all members of the work team and for increasing team cohesion.

Designing Training Systems to Address Age-Related Differences

We began this chapter by describing best practices for developing training that fits the needs of organizations and employees. We've also discussed the ways in which age issues may intersect with the design of training programs. In this section we provide a summary guide for developing training programs of particular relevance for late-career learners.

Training Needs Assessment

The needs assessment process is where one uncovers what is needed to fit the training to the needs of the organization and its employees. Thus, it's an opportunity to better understand what if any issues related to aging are relevant to your workforce, such as level of interest in training and self-confidence in learning ability. Training needs assessment is also important to get a read of the organizational culture, specifically whether the organizational culture supports people of all ages in gaining new skills. This is also a time to be sure that trainers – and everyone in the organization for that matter – sets aside any biases about what an "older learner" is like or what they are interested in or capable of.

Trainee Characteristics and Contextual Issues

Training is not "one size fits all". Before embarking on a training program, consider the fit between your training program and trainee and organizational characteristics. Special Focus Box 4.2 gives some tips about this issue.

Special Focus Box 4.2: Fit the Training Program to the Learner – Regardless of Age!

Training methods should be flexible and fit the needs of learners of all types – including those of different age and education levels. Here are some issues to consider.

- Does the training use jargon that some employees may not understand? Does it use language and readings appropriate for all education levels? If pictures are used in the training, are images of learners of all ages and backgrounds included as well?
- Training programs are most effective when they minimize trainee differences by letting to work at their own pace. Can older workers review aspects of training that may already be familiar to them?
- Are trainees motivated to learn and participate in the specific training program? How will the program be introduced to trainees (e.g., remediation for poor performers? an opportunity for development?) How relevant are the skills to be trained to the trainee? If the topic is not inherently interesting, what can be done to get the trainee motivated?
- Learner self-efficacy is critical. Do trainees perceive themselves as able to learn? How can you increase self-efficacy? Early training experiences can shape training self-efficacy. This might mean providing training in small, bite-sized pieces to enhance confidence.
- Feedback is essential (see Chapter 8). Learners need frequent, progress-oriented feedback in order to correct their mistakes quickly and to adjust their strategy and effort. While feedback is important for everyone, it's especially important for learners who are less able to assess whether they are mastering the material.

- Organizational culture around training has a large but often underappreciated influence on learning. Does the organization value investing in all of its members, including older workers? Does the culture support transfer of training back to the workplace?
- Tying training content to existing knowledge can help workers learn more quickly, especially for experienced learners who can build on their current job knowledge.
- Consider who is likely to learn best with each training approach. Given the variability among older adults in terms of interest and ability to learn (typically more than among younger age groups; see Chapter 5) it's important to consider the climate for learning.
- Similarly, feedback should be personally meaningful to learners and expressed in ways that are useful to them. For example, telling a learner that they are doing better than they did last time is more helpful than telling them how they did relative to others.
- Because late-career employees have greater accumulated knowledge and may be more motivated by the work itself, social interaction, and giving back (see Chapter 3), they could be considered a valuable resource as trainers and mentors to junior colleagues. In addition, "reverse mentoring" relationships promote knowledge sharing and learning in both directions across age groups. We talk more about mentoring and other career development strategies in Chapter 8.

Choosing Training Methods

Which training method or methods are used are partly determined by the skills that need to be trained and by organizational resources. In addition, certain training methods are more beneficial for situations where flexibility is needed to address the needs of different learners. For example:

- **On-the-job training** can allow people to learn at their own pace.
- **A classroom setting** can be useful for teaching information and concepts, but it should be used with care if a goal is to make age differences less salient to learners.
- Similarly, much **online training**, because it is often segmented into modules, can allow for the tailoring of learning to individual learner needs and also allow learners to go at their own pace – very quickly, or more slowly if it suits their needs. Many online systems also provide

feedback to learners on how well they are doing. Online training also does not make age differences salient to learners.

- Watching **models** actually performing the tasks (either live or video) emphasizes the job-relevance of the training, enhancing trainee motivation to learn and self-efficacy.

Evaluation of the Training

Obviously, organizations may expect some sort of evaluation of the training program given the investment in the training. The detailed discussion of training evaluations is beyond the scope of this book. However, in the context of age differences, we make two strong suggestions. First, trainee reactions to the training, especially in terms of whether they found the training to be valuable, should be assessed. That is because when trainees see training as job-relevant, they are more likely to transfer it to the job.[7] And training that is seen as relevant is key to increasing trainee motivation. Second, it can be highly valuable to get information from trainees about how they experienced the training process. This could be as simple as interviewing trainees, perhaps while the training process is ongoing. This can help making a course correction while it is still possible to do so, or at least to change the training next time that it is delivered.[8]

Summary

Ironically, we argue that the development of training programs to support older learners begins with the assumption that older workers are not that different from their younger colleagues. Nor should one assume that all older workers are essentially alike. While there are some issues that may be particular to older learners, these are characteristics shared by many younger learners as well. Plus, there is considerable variability among older workers, such as in their motivation to learn, ability, and technological savvy. Rather, the goal should be a training program focused on the established best practices and research about what works for the broadest range of learners. Put differently, developing a training program that can be sufficiently flexible to address age-related differences is the one that will also tend to address all learners' needs – regardless of their age.

The PIERA Approach to Developing a Training Program That Addresses the Needs of Late-Career Workers

We encourage you to reflect on the ideas in this chapter in light of your own organization or team(s), using the PIERA structure to develop or upskill your current team. In this section we give you a number of ideas for how to approach this. As always, we encourage you to take on something that makes sense for you, your organization, and its resources and culture.

Planning

- What is the skill or competency that you think is missing and needs to be trained? Is it a skill that is modifiable through practice? What would training success look like? How would new skill learning that is transferred back onto the job affect the team or unit's performance?
- What are the current skill level of the target skill on your team? How does this differ across individual members? How comfortable or interested is each team member in learning the target skill? Are there major differences between early- and late-career employees, such as in their education, current skills, or self-confidence? Keep in mind that good training practices that are relevant for a wide range of people in general will likely address many of the issues associated with older learners as well.
- What are the skills and abilities needed to perform the job's tasks?
- What is the current knowledge and performance levels of employees? Specific indicators of a need for training should guide the development of the program.
- What organizational resources are available for training and development?
- What is the culture of the organization with regard to training? The team? In particular, is training valued by the organization and by the team? What factors may inhibit transfer of learned skills back to the job?
- Is investment in late-career employees valued by the organization?
- It is highly recommended that you work with employees (and managers) to get a better feel for the key issues and to be sure your analysis is correct. Not only does this help to get a training approach that "fits", it also gains employee support. You may consider having conversations with individuals and with the team to gauge reactions. Resistance from employees should be a red flag, and employee involvement can reduce such resistance.
- Once your data are gathered and reviewed, consider how these issues might be addressed. List out very clear and specific characteristics, goals, and objectives for your pilot training and how they would address the needs of your team or organization. Also, what training methods make

the most sense for the training content, learners, and available budget? How will you measure success of the program?

Implementation

Here is an example of a specific, small-scale training program. This example is very specific to this organization, and the particular training program would depend on the results of the planning stage. In other words, any program should be tailored to the particular organization.

In this simple example, the goal of the training is to address changes in the redesign of restaurant space, specifically for servers, to address new health regulations introduced to deal with infectious disease (e.g., COVID-19) or new state regulations. Note that this is a high-end restaurant that has been around for many years. While it does have younger servers, it also has late-career servers who have worked at the restaurant for decades and have a substantial "following" among the clientele.

The objectives of this example training program are to:

- Familiarize workers with knowledge of the new regulations and procedures on handling of food. This would include washing of hands and proper handling of utensils coming from and returning to the kitchen. Preparing for this new system and its implementation would require some employee and management input. It may also require some redesign of the workplace and the purchasing of new equipment.
- Teach. servers about how the space will be redesigned to address the new state regulations and how this will impact what they actually do on the job.

Prior to the start of this program, a short bullet-list of reasons describing the state regulations behind this program behind this redesign of work will be provided to the team.

The training will have several parts:

- Preliminary meetings with employees explaining the regulations, the redesign of work, and what they will need to learn.
- State-provided online training about the new safety regulations and how these will affect employees. This is broken up into modules such that employees can work at their own pace and are given feedback on what they have mastered and where they need additional work.
- On-the-job training by supervisors, with workers observing behavior of both supervisors and each other, which will also allow for questions and answers from trainees.

Note that procedures will be put into place to evaluate the approach midstream to decide if it needs adjustment. For example, do workers even understand and agree with the new regulations? Do they feel able to handle the new job tasks? Is there any employee or supervisor resistance? If so, why, and what can be done?

Evaluation

- All employees will have to reach a minimum score on the online training provided by the state.
- Two weeks after implementation, reactions will be assessed by means of team discussions and discussions with clientele. This will also help gauge whether each objective is perceived to have been accomplished.

Reflection

- Prior to compiling the data, the team leader should reflect on their own about their perception of how they believed things changed from the original discussion of the changes to the period after the training has taken place. Did any palpable change occur? Was behavior consistent over the month, or did employees revert back to their old behaviors? Did unexpected things happen? Understanding these issues could help with further implementation in other parts of the organization.
- Once the data are compiled, the leader should look for trends. Do the data from employees and customers mirror the leader's own reflections? Where are there inconsistencies? Is anything jumping out at you as particularly successful or problematic?
- Following a private reflection and notes, the data can be shared with the team in a digestible format. What are their reactions? Do they agree with the data? Can they help you interpret and issues with implementation and how to solve them? An open discussion period should be scheduled once they have a chance to reflect carefully. Also, the leader should be available for private discussions with individual team members as well.

Adjustment

- Based on the reflection period, a meeting can be scheduled to take suggestions for adjusting the intervention based its level of success. If the training didn't quite work, or it only worked for some people, or it didn't "stick", how can it be approached in a different manner?
- If there was more success than failure, how can this pilot be used to implement more permanent changes? Are their lessons learned in this team that could inform other teams or other levels of the organization?

Action Items: Things to Do Right Now, Next Week, and Long Term...

Things to Do Right Now

Skim back over the chapter and any notes you took. Did anything jump out at you as something you hadn't thought about before when you've considered training and development? Which points deserve further consideration for you or your own team? Write those down.

Things to Do Next Week

Think about some of the people on your team who have been in the organization for a while. Do you have a good idea of what training or development they may need? What kind of training and development would be of interest to them? Can you find some time next week to schedule any needed one-on-ones with members of your team to check in to see how their interests and goals may be shifting and to think about what types of development opportunities might be most relevant for those team members?

Things to Do Long Term

Are you aware of whether HR in your organization provides training opportunities for all employees regardless of their age? Even if HR says that they do, would people of all ages in the organization agree with this? Can you think of ways to communicate the value of training people of all ages to the organization's leadership? Who can help with this?

Notes

1. Bell, B. S., Tannenbaum, S. I., Ford, J. K., Noe, R. A., & Kraiger, K. (2017). 100 years of training and development research: What we know and where we should go. *Journal of Applied Psychology, 102*, 305–323; Goldstein, I. L., & Ford, J. K. (2002). *Training in organizations: Needs assessment, development, and evaluation* (4th ed.). Belmont, CA: Wadsworth Cengage Learning; Noe, R. A., Clarke, A. D., & Klein, H. J. (2014). Learning in the twenty-first-century workplace. *Annual Review of Organizational Psychology and Organizational Behavior, 1*, 245–275; Salas, E., Tannenbaum, S. I., Kraiger, K., & Smith-Jentsch, K. A. (2012). The science of training and development in organizations: What matters in practice. *Psychological Science in the Public Interest, 13*, 74–101.

2. Ng, T. W., & Feldman, D. C. (2012). Evaluating six common stereotypes about older workers with meta-analytical data. *Personnel Psychology, 65,* 821–858.

3. Kooij, D. T., De Lange, A. H., Jansen, P. G., Kanfer, R., & Dikkers, J. S. (2011). Age and work-related motives: Results of a meta-analysis. *Journal of Organizational Behavior, 32,* 197–225; Zaniboni, S., Truxillo, D. M., & Fraccaroli, F. (2013). Differential effects of task variety and skill variety on burnout and turnover intentions for older and younger workers. *European Journal of Work and Organizational Psychology, 22,* 306–317.

4. Boehm, S. A., Kunze, F., & Bruch, H. (2014). Spotlight on age-diversity climate: The impact of age-inclusive HR practices on firm-level outcomes. *Personnel Psychology, 67,* 667–704.

5. Beier, M. E., Teachout, M. S., & Cox, C. B. (2012). The training and development of an aging workforce. In *The Oxford handbook of work and aging* (pp. 436–453). Oxford University Press.

6. Kanfer, R., & Ackerman, P. L. (2004). Aging, adult development, and work motivation. *Academy of Management Review, 29,* 440–458; Kooij, D. T., De Lange, A. H., Jansen, P. G., Kanfer, R., & Dikkers, J. S. (2011). Age and work-related motives: Results of a meta-analysis. *Journal of Organizational Behavior, 32,* 197–225; Zaniboni, S., Truxillo, D. M., & Fraccaroli, F. (2013). Differential effects of task variety and skill variety on burnout and turnover intentions for older and younger workers. *European Journal of Work and Organizational Psychology, 22,* 306–317.

7. Alliger, G. M., Tannenbaum, S. I., Bennett Jr, W., Traver, H., & Shotland, A. (1997). A meta-analysis of the relations among training criteria. *Personnel Psychology, 50,* 341–358.

8. Beier, M. E., Teachout, M. S., & Cox, C. B. (2012). The training and development of an aging workforce. In *The Oxford handbook of work and aging* (pp. 436–453); Czaja, S. J., & Sharit, J. (2012). *Designing training and instructional programs for older adults.* CRC Press; Kraiger, K. (2017). Designing effective training for older workers. In *The Palgrave handbook of age diversity and work* (pp. 639–667). London: Palgrave Macmillan.

Adjusting to Changes in Workers' Physical and Other Abilities over Time

5

Although several rapidly growing sectors of the economy such as information technology do not demand high levels of physical ability, an employee's physical health and skill continues to play an important role in employability for many jobs.[1] The effects of aging on work outcomes depends on two important factors: (1) the physical and cognitive demands of the job, and (2) employee capability to meet job demands. In this chapter we discuss how age-related changes in general and individual differences in particular may affect work ability in different types of jobs. We also discuss what organizations can actually do to support work ability.

With aging, people change in a number of ways. While some of these changes do not affect work, others do. For example, as we have discussed, job performance changes little with age, and there may even be improvements in some job behaviors like safety. There is also an improvement in job attitudes like job satisfaction. Of course, there are some declines as well. For instance, for physically demanding jobs (e.g., construction) or for highly cognitively demanding jobs (e.g., air traffic controller), some age-related changes may make it difficult for people to do their jobs. Plus, there are jobs that have *both* a heavy cognitive and a heavy physical component: For example, nursing requires not only a knowledge of medical practices and patient care, but also may require physical tasks such as lifting and moving patients.

But age-related changes vary considerably across individuals and may or may not manifest in work outcomes depending on the particular situation. First, while there are some general trends in people's abilities over time – most people experience decreased physical ability or have normal, minor cognitive declines – different people age differently. One worker may be fully capable of continuing their work until late in life, while others will find that they have to modify their job during mid-career or quit. Second, differences in the type of work can obviously interact to affect an individual's ability to continue working. For example, a worker in a sedentary job may be better able to continue working into later life than a worker in a job that requires heavy lifting.

The focus of this chapter is to describe the types of physical, cognitive, and other changes that take place within the person across the work lifespan and how they may affect the performance, attitudes, and health of workers. We begin by describing changes that most people experience as they age and how these changes impact the workplace. We also describe the concept of *work ability* and how it can help workers and managers understand and address what different people may need to continue in their jobs. We conclude with a discussion of what adjustments can be made to jobs from the perspective of both managers and employees, applying the PIERA approach to developing a plan to support late-career workers.

Aging Brings Some Losses – But Also Some Gains

For most people, aging is associated with some physical and cognitive losses. Some of these may be quite minor, whereas others can impair a person in significant ways. And some of these losses are more easily addressed than others. For example, a person may find that they develop issues with reading small print, an issue easily addressed with reading glasses. However, others losses may be more significant, such as a back injury that seriously limits mobility. One way of looking at this is that, as we age, we tend to accumulate a number of disabilities, some minor and some significant. And the number of accumulated disabilities begins to accelerate for the population as a whole at around age 50.[2] Although people differ in terms of the nature of these losses and how quickly they happen, physical and mental losses can produce challenges for people who can or must continue working – as well as for their employers and for society. Let's discuss these different types of age-related losses and why they may or may not matter for a person's work.

Physical Losses

Perhaps the age-related physical losses are the most salient. For example, there can be losses such physical strength, hearing, and aerobic capacity. Further, there is frequently some decline in the ability to maintain homeostasis, that is, for a person's body to return back to normal after environmental changes such as extreme temperatures. This may make it more difficult for older workers to work under physically extreme conditions.[3] Sleep disturbances that come with aging add to adjusting to shift work. There are also increases in pain and in some physical ailments.[4] Plus, older bodies may take longer to recover from injuries.[5] Obviously, these can all hinder the ability to do certain types of work, especially work that is physically demanding.

Cognitive Losses

Similarly, there are also some losses in cognitive abilities. Starting at about age 20, fluid cognitive abilities – related to things like the ability to quickly process information as well as working memory – begin a gradual decline.[6] These changes may increase for people in their 60s, although there are differences across individuals as to how quickly these changes occur.

But These Losses May Not Negatively Affect a Person's Work

Given these declines, it is often assumed – erroneously – that a person's job performance and attitudes will decline as they age. But the research does not bear this out. For example, people's performance of core tasks in most jobs seems fairly stable over time or may show only small decreases.[7] On the other hand, there seem to be some performance dimensions that improve with age, such as increased safety behaviors and reduced accidents.[8] Similarly, older workers may show increases in what is called "organizational citizenship behavior", like helping coworkers or the team. They also tend to have fewer sickness absences, and their job attitudes – things like job satisfaction and commitment – generally seem to improve.

Why are many of the losses that experienced by older people not reflected on the job? There are several reasons. First, most jobs do not require maximum utilization of our physical and cognitive skills at all times.[9] For example, with a few exceptions (like air traffic controller), most jobs do not require the maximum use of our fluid intelligence skills at all times. For experienced workers (who learned the job often years before), job tasks have become routinized and so not require high levels of cognitive attention; that is, the tasks become habitual like driving. That means that common age-related cognitive losses would not be expected to affect the worker's performance unless the losses become severe or the job changes in a way that prevents the use of routine actions.

The second reason that aging is not uniformly related to declining job performance is that different people age differently. That is, while there may be some declines in many people, this is not necessarily true for everyone (see Special Focus Box 5.1 for more on this). People also differ in the rate of decline, with some people for example showing relatively little memory loss well into their 80s, while others show early signs of memory loss in their 60s. Third, people often change the way they do their work to work "smarter". For example, a person who has been doing their job for many years and finds that they are less able to do certain aspects of it may find workarounds. Those might include

---

Special Focus Box 5.1: Aging Differently = Greater Variability

As we have emphasized throughout this book, there are as many differences *within* age groups as there are between age groups. For instance, within a group of 24-year-olds there are quite a few differences in cognitive ability and physical abilities. Similarly, you will also find a lot of differences in cognitive and physical abilities within a group of 65-year-olds. And we also know that the average scores on these abilities tend to be lower in older groups.

What also changes with age, though, is the *range* of differences on these abilities. For example, consider the scores on a test of mental processing speed. The average score on this test will probably be lower in a group of older people compared with the average score in a group of younger people. However, there will be bigger differences between the lowest and highest score in the older group. Because people age differently – they age at different speeds – the older group would contain people who have changed little since they were young. But it will also contain people who might be experiencing significant cognitive declines. A similar pattern would also be expected for other abilities such as physical abilities.

trading off certain tasks with other workers or finding ways to redesign their work (crafting their job, as we describe in Chapter 3). Fourth, a person might be assigned by their employer to a position that is more in keeping with their current strengths and abilities. Fifth, the number of jobs that require high levels of physical skill is declining in many industrialized countries, suggesting that the physical requirements of many jobs may be fewer these days, at least mitigating the effects of the age-related physical declines. For example, the adoption of new technologies has reduced the lifting demands in warehouse work. Sixth, many of the most serious age-related declines occur much later in life, after the standard retirement age. For example, declines that could impact work performance for most jobs typically occur in later old age, and even then, there is a great deal of variability. Finally, it is important to know that people may experience some gains as they age. We discuss these in the next section.

Gains and Resources that Come with Age

Although many people focus on the declines that come with aging, particularly physical ability losses, there are important cognitive gains. First, as we noted before, while there are declines in fluid intelligence, this is only half the story: With age also come gains is what is known as crystallized cognitive abilities, sometimes described as the accumulated knowledge and wisdom that translates into job skills. Crystallized cognitive abilities typically increase throughout a person's entire working life. Second, there are also thought to be some positive changes in personality that occur as a person ages. For example, neuroticism – which includes negative thoughts about oneself and about others – appears to decline. This may be why older people tend to describe themselves as "feeling more comfortable in their own skin". This may also explain some of the increases in job satisfaction. People also appear to become more conscientious – focused on accomplishment and orderliness – and conscientiousness is one of the most important personality traits for work performance, particularly organizational citizenship and safety. Third, there seems to be a greater focus on building strong interpersonal relationships at work as people age, which may also support organizational citizenship. Older workers may also focus more on intrinsic motivation (wanting to do the work for the sake of the work itself) and exhibit increased generativity motives (the desire to give back to future generations), an issue discussed in Chapter 3.[10]

The Work Context Can Affect a Person's "Work Ability" – and What You Can Do About That

In the previous sections, we've mostly discussed the age-related changes that might affect work performance. But this is only half the story, as it's well established that behavior and attitudes are also significantly influenced by a person's work environment. *In other words, an employee's performance, well-being, and attitudes at work are a function not only of the person themselves, but also the intersection of the person and their job.*

That is where the PIERA approach and the concept of *work ability* (defined below) come in. Together, they can help policy-makers, employers, and workers themselves think about what they can do to change their work environment, both in terms of both the physical and social work environment to keep people happy and productive throughout their lifespans. Perhaps the most important factor here is to consider how analyzing a work situation from the standpoint of work ability can be used to support people at different career stages.

What Is Work Ability?

Work ability is a concept that initially emerged in the occupational medicine literature. Developed by Finnish researcher Juhani Ilmarinen in the 1980s, work ability was conceptualized as how well a person can meet the requirements of their job. The original measure of work ability focused on the number of serious medical diagnoses a person has had in combination with their own beliefs about how well they are meeting the physical and psychological aspects of their work.[11]

What was significant about this initial research is that it found that work ability is a good predictor of important outcomes like whether a person will later go on disability. Relevant to the present discussion is that work ability also predicted the likelihood that a person would retire – a finding that has been borne out by a recent meta-analysis.[12] Also, work ability generally declined as people age, although, not surprisingly, this was most pronounced for people in blue-collar (i.e., physically demanding) jobs.[13] A central point is that the researchers found that a person's work ability is affected not only by changes in the person but was also influenced by their context. *That is, age-related changes in work ability are a function not only of the person but of the job itself.*

Given the strength of the work ability concept, researchers who study aging at work have tried to understand more about what work ability is and how to measure it. First, it is generally agreed that work ability is *a person's ability to meet the physical and mental requirements of their job*. Second, many researchers have recently moved towards short measures of "perceived work ability" that do not require any physical diagnosis on the part of a physician. This more recent research has generally found that these non-medical measures of work ability provide much of the same information as the medically focused measures and can be administered to employees much more easily. See Special Focus Box 5.2 for measurement ideas.

Special Focus Box 5.2: What Is Your Work Ability?

There are a number of measures of work ability. Some measures that take into account a person's actual health and whether they have been diagnosed with an illness. However, one of the most popular measures of perceived work ability is quite simple – only four items – which are as follows:

1. What is your current work ability compared with your lifetime best?
2. How do you rate your current work ability with respect to the mental demands of your job?
3. How do you rate your current work ability with respect to the physical demands of your job?
4. How do you rate your current work ability with respect to the interpersonal demands of your job?

These items are rated on a scale of 0 (completely unable to work) to 10 (work ability at its best) and then averaged. Although there is no standard, "accepted" level of work ability on this scale, it does relate to important variables such as retirement.

Brady, G. M., Truxillo, D. M., Cadiz, D. M., Rineer, J. R., Caughlin, D. E., & Bodner, T. (2020). Opening the black box: Examining the nomological network of work ability and its role in organizational research. *Journal of Applied Psychology, 105*, 637–670.

Ilmarinen, J., Tuomi, K., Eskelinen, L., Nygård, C. H., Huuhtanen, P., & Klockars, M. (1991). Background and objectives of the Finnish research project on aging workers in municipal occupations. *Scandinavian Journal of Work, Environment & Health, 17*, 7–11.

McGonagle, A. K., Fisher, G. G., Barnes-Farrell, J. L., & Grosch, J. W. (2015). Individual and work factors related to perceived work ability and labor force outcomes. *Journal of Applied Psychology, 100*, 376–398.

Why Does Work Ability Matter?

We now know a lot about the outcomes of work ability – why it matters – as well as what can be done to improve a person's work ability. A recent meta-analysis summarized hundreds of studies involving hundreds of thousands of workers over the last 30 years. We show a graphical version of this study's findings in Figure 5.1. In this section we specifically focus on the why work ability matters (its outcomes, in the right-hand box) as well as the factors that organizations and employees can consider to boost work ability (the left-hand box).

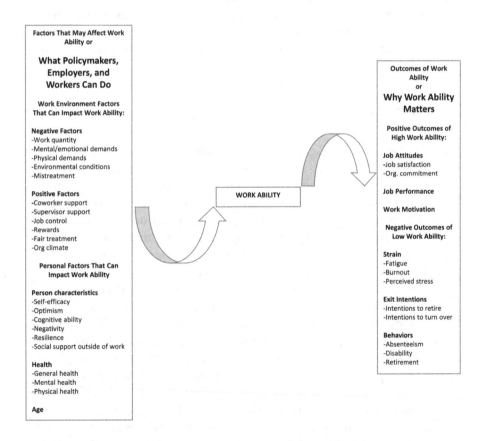

Figure 5.1   Factors that can affect work ability and why work ability matters

(Based on: Brady, G. M., Truxillo, D. M., Cadiz, D. M., Rineer, J. R., Caughlin, D. E., & Bodner, T. (2020). Opening the black box: Examining the nomological network of work ability and its role in organizational research. *Journal of Applied Psychology, 105*, 637–670.)

First, work ability matters for both employers and employees. As you can see in Figure 5.1, the meta-analysis found that work ability relates to outcomes that organizations care about such as improved job attitudes. That is, employees with higher work ability tended to have higher job satisfaction and commitment to the organization. Even more compelling from an organization's perspective was that work ability was related to greater employee motivation and job performance as well as to lower absenteeism, disability claims; and among older workers, it was related not only to decreased intentions to retire and actual retirement. Finally, work ability was related to important well-being outcomes like employee fatigue, burnout, and stress. Taken together, these results show that from the viewpoint of both employers and workers, work ability matters. In fact, we would argue that for these reasons work ability is a factor that should matter not only to employees and employers but to policy-makers and governments as well.

What Can Be Done to Boost Work Ability?

As can also be seen in Figure 5.1, there are a number of factors, both positive and negative, that relate to work ability as well. Of course, an employee's physical and mental health is related to their work ability. And a number of other personal factors – things like a person's resilience, optimism, and support outside of work can have a positive impact on their work ability. But there are many workplace issues that can have an impact as well. For example, a number of negative factors such as having too much work, overly high demands (e.g., having too many responsibilities at once that are difficult to prioritize), and physical demands can negatively affect work ability. And of course negative environmental conditions (e.g., excessive noise) can hurt work ability and may pose safety and health risks as well. In the most recent COVID-19 pandemic, for example, older workers with preexisting conditions may experience greater apprehension about returning to the workplace, potentially having a negative impact on their work ability.[14]

At the same time there are other workplace factors that may not be obvious at first but that can affect work ability. For example, mistreatment at work can negatively impact a person's work ability. And there are many workplace factors that are related to higher work ability: support from coworkers, support from supervisors, greater control over work, rewards, a positive climate, and fair treatment. *In other words, even organizations that don't think they can significantly redesign the way that their work is carried out can at least create a supportive work environment with a positive climate and fair treatment*. Interestingly, while age was found to have a negative impact on work ability (i.e., as one might expect, work ability seems to decline with age), its effects on work ability were not that strong; workplace factors had much stronger effects!

Although many of the person characteristics that affect work ability – such as health – may seem out of the control of the organization, is not necessarily true. For example, there are a number of work context issues – such as support and fair treatment – that have been shown to affect a person's physical and mental health.[15] In fact, the National Institute for Occupational Safety and Health (NIOSH) provides a number of best practices for employers. Specifically, NIOSH notes that as part of its Total Worker Health ® (TWH) initiative that the work itself and the work environment – both within the control of the employer – affect workers' health.

We also note that many of the factors that affect work ability may be affected by work ability as well. For example, a person with high work ability may end up becoming more optimistic, and vice-versa. Second, by the same token, the items we describe as outcomes of work ability may also affect work ability as well. For example, a person with high work ability will probably be a high performer, and the feedback that they are high performing employee may increase their work ability. Third, we also note that there are a number of factors that have not been researched for their impacts on work ability. One obvious example is age discrimination. As we discuss in Chapter 6, age discrimination and its pernicious cousin negative age climate, both are likely to have a negative effect on an individual's work ability. Although this specific issue has not yet been examined, preliminary research does suggest that employees who experience workplace discrimination also have lower work ability.[16] Finally, we note that the model we present here can be useful to consider for workers at all career stages, but may become particularly important when managing late-career employees who are dealing with age-related declines in certain physical abilities. An example might be late-career teachers with co-morbidities who, in the recent pandemic, had to decide whether to return to the classroom.

Examples of How to Implement Changes in the Workplace to Support Work Ability

The research shows that work ability affects a number of outcomes like attitudes, motivation, well-being, and behavior. These are all outcomes that are important to workers, as well as to organizations and to society. Redesigning the physical environment, even in simple ways, can have a profound effect on work ability. Major changes to the physical design of work may not be possible for some employers, but sometimes a bit of careful diagnosis can inspire ways to improve the workplace at relatively low cost. Before we get into applying the PIERA approach to enhancing work ability, we look to current research on age in the workplace for ideas on how employers and workers themselves might improve work ability.

Below are just a few examples of types of workplace interventions that have been used to support late-career workers. It is important to note a few things. First, some interventions focus on the physical aspects of the job, while others provide support to the social environment. Second, while some may have originally been developed to support late-career workers, most interventions will likely help workers of all ages. Third, some of these examples may seem fairly substantial (e.g., redesigning a factory), but many others are much more straightforward and within the reach of most employers.

- Some employers are redesigning the workplace to reduce physical demands, especially if they have a highly experienced and skilled workforce that they want to retain. In the late 2000s, German auto-maker BMW was just such an employer: They realized that their highly skilled workforce was aging, and that the average age of their workforce would rise from 39 in 2007 to 47 in 2017, and they wanted to maintain this accumulated "human capital". BMW also assessed their employees' work ability, finding that while work ability decreased with age, there was quite a bit of variability – some workers remained quite productive. They set about trying to find relatively straightforward ways to address these age-related changes by doing a study on making workplace changes. They staffed one of their production lines with workers with an average age of 47, that is, the mean age they expected their workforce to be in 2017. They then took a "bottom-up" approach, working with employees on the line along with managers and technical experts. Some of the changes were physical, like using wooden flooring and new footwear to decrease wear-and-tear on workers' joints, and installing work stations that could be adjusted for an individual employee's height. They added ergonomic chairs so employees could sit if need be. They also added job rotation to balance out the physical load on workers, and they included strength and stretching exercises in the work day. The new production line increased productivity by 7%.[17]

- An example of a technological redesign (e.g., robotics and other technology to help with lifting) combined with a fitness program comes from Maine's outdoor clothing and equipment outfitter, L.L. Bean. In this case, the company realized that older workers can face health and safety risks in physically demanding jobs. Because their average employee age was 50, meaning that many of them would be developing musculoskeletal problems, L.L. Bean set about to rethink their work. First, they used technological approaches. These included a combination of vacuum-driven lift-assist devices and robotics that reduced the need for heavy lifting by individuals. They also introduced a voluntary fitness program. The company estimated that due to things like reduced workers' compensation cases and medical costs, there was a cost-avoidance of $3.15 for each dollar they spent on the program. Notably, these changes were ones that benefit not only older workers, but workers of all ages.[18]

- Other workplace approaches may be geared towards a specific profession. For example, nursing is a job that often requires a good bit of physical strength. A particular challenge can be moving or turning patients, which is associated with nurse injuries. This is especially an issue given that the nurse workforce is aging. One solution used by many healthcare organizations is safe patient handling equipment, which allows the nurse to move or turn a patient without significant lifting on their part. A recent meta-analysis of 27 studies found that this equipment leads to significant reductions in injuries.[19]

- Depending on the work, employers can give employees the latitude to do some aspects of their jobs in their own way as long as the work gets done. Late career workers may be especially good at redesigning their work in this way. For example, employers can train workers on how to "craft" their jobs to perform it most effectively, working with supervisors and coworkers as a team. This may be especially useful to helping workers adapt to age-related changes. This approach is also consistent with the idea that as people age they need to focus on particular skills and tasks to optimize their performance and compensate for any losses. This might also allow these more seasoned employees to "craft" their jobs to fit their own current needs, in concert with their coworkers and supervisors (as we mention in Chapter 3). For example, one study in Germany found that older nurses who were given control over their work and who focused on ways to optimize their work experienced greater work ability.[20]

- It is also important to treat people of all ages fairly. As shown in Figure 5.1, fair treatment affects work ability. Fair treatment has also been consistently shown to affect performance, health, and well-being.[21] And it is the right thing to do.
- Relatedly, it is important to develop HR practices – such as hiring, promotion, training opportunities, performance appraisal, and pay – that treat all employees fairly at different ages and career stages. These types of practices build a positive age diversity climate, and they can enhance organizational performance as well. As one compelling example, a study of 93 German companies found that age-friendly HR practices, where people of all ages are given the same opportunities, led to a positive age diversity climate, which in turn led to increased company performance and reduced intentions to quit among workers. In other words, age-inclusive HR practices lead to a positive age climate leading to important benefits – for workers of all ages.[22]
- Supervisor and coworker support are important for work ability. This might be enhanced through training supervisors and team members to foster support for each other. For lasting results, it is also important to build this kind of support from top management on down.

Example: The PIERA Approach to Supporting Work Ability

We encourage you to reflect on the ideas in this chapter in light of your own organization or team(s), using the PIERA structure to support employees' work ability. In this section we give you a number of ideas for how to approach this. As always, we encourage you to take on something that makes sense for you, your organization, and its resources and culture.

Planning

- What is the current "work ability" of your team? How does this differ across individual members? Keep in mind that work ability is not only an issue for people in highly physical jobs, but for those in other job types as well, including those that might be considered highly sedentary. For example, call center employees are considered to have some health risks *because* the job is so sedentary.[23] In addition, work ability is not only an issue for people in their late careers, but is also a factor that likely develops over time.
- Are there any specific outcomes of work ability (the right-hand box in Figure 5.1), such as job attitudes, performance, or stress, that are signs that work ability may be an issue in this group?

- What are some of the factors that may be affecting your employees' work ability? Look at the factors in Figure 5.1 under "Factors that May Affect Work Ability" for guidance.
- It is highly recommended that you work with employees (and managers) to get a better feel for the key issues and to be sure your analysis is correct. Note that in the BMW case, one important part of its success was that it included significant input from employees from the start. This also helps to gain employee support. You may consider having conversations with individuals and with the team to gauge reactions. Significant resistance from employees could doom the program, and employee involvement can reduce such resistance.
- Once your data are gathered and reviewed, do you have a better sense of what might be driving any problems you were seeing? How might these issues be addressed? List out very clear and specific objectives for your pilot intervention.

Implementation

Here is an example of a specific, small-scale intervention to help support work ability for certain types of workers. This example is very specific to this organization, and the particular intervention would depend on the results of the planning stage. In other words, any program should be tailored to the particular organization.

In this simple example, the goal is to address the work ability of sedentary office workers. This would require input and buy-in from employees.

The objectives of this example work ability intervention for sedentary employees are to:

- Redesign the workplace with sit-stand desks. This would include some training in how to use the desks. Preparing for this solution and its implementation might require some employee and management input on the type of desks and trying out a number of different types of desks. It may mean that different employees could choose the type of sit-stand desk that they want.
- Encourage workers to take mini-breaks periodically to move around and stretch. This would require input on what would get employees to actually take these breaks and move around.

Prior to the start of this program, a short bullet-list of reasons describing why this program is being tested out will be provided to the team. Dates will be scheduled for implementation of the desks and the trainings. The meetings will have a specific start and stop time that will be respected and will have a clear agenda.

- Procedures will be put into place to evaluate the approach midstream to decide if it needs adjustment, perhaps 1 week after implementation. For example, do employees know how to use the desks? Are they actually using the sit-stand function? If not, why not? (e.g., are the desks hard to use?) Are they actually taking their breaks? If not, why not? (e.g., is there excessive workload?) Is there any employee or supervisor resistance? If so, why?

Evaluation

- One month after implementation, reactions will be assessed by means of team discussions and brief, anonymous electronic survey. This will also help gauge whether each objective is perceived to have been accomplished.

Reflection

- Prior to compiling the data, the team leader should reflect on their own about their perception of how they believed things changed over the course of the month. Did any palpable change occur? Was it consistent over the month, or did it die down after a honeymoon period? Did unexpected things happen? Understanding these issues could help with further implementation in other parts of the organization.
- Once the data are compiled, the leader should look for trends. Do the data mirror the leaders own reflections? Where are there inconsistencies? Is anything jumping out at you as particularly successful or problematic?
- Following a private reflection and notes, the data can be shared with the team in a digestible format. What are their reactions? Do they agree with the data? Can they help you interpret and issues with implementation and how to solve them? An open discussion period should be scheduled once they have a chance to reflect carefully. Also, the leader should be available for private discussions with individual team members as well.

Adjustment

- Based on the reflection period, a meeting can be scheduled to take suggestions for adjusting the intervention based its level of success. If the intervention didn't quite work, how can it be approached in a different manner?
- If there was more success than failure, how can this pilot be used to implement more permanent changes? Are their lessons learned in this team that could inform other teams or other levels of the organization?

**Action Items: Things to Do Right Now,
Next Week, and Long Term …**

Things to Do Right Now

Skim back over the chapter and any notes you took. Did anything jump out at you as something you hadn't thought about before when you've considered people's changing skills and abilities and how this might affect their ability to continue working? Which points deserve further consideration for you or your own team? Write those down.

Things to Do Next Week

Think about some of the people on your team who have been in the organization for a while. Do you have a good idea of what their level of work ability might be? What might be done to help support their work ability? Can you find some time next week to schedule any needed one-on-ones with members of your team to check in to see what they think they need, and what skills they might share with others on the team?

Things to Do Long Term

Are you aware of whether HR in your organization provides any kind of support to keep their best talent regardless of their age? Even if HR says that they do, would people of all ages in the organization agree with this? Can you think of ways to communicate the value of supporting people of all ages to preserve their ability to work effectively and so that the organization can retain this talent? Who can help with communicating this?

Notes

1. Pew Research Center. (2016). *The state of American jobs*. Available at: https://www.pewsocialtrends.org/2016/10/06/1-changes-in-the-american-workplace/
2. Bruyère, S. (2006). Disability management: Key concepts and techniques for an aging workforce. *International Journal of Disability Management Research, 1*, 149–158; Kampfe, C. M., Wadsworth, J. S., Mamboleo, G. I., & Schonbrun, S. L. (2008). Aging, disability, and employment. *Work, 31*, 337–344.

3. McDonald, R. B. (1988). The physiological aspects of aging. In H. Dennis (Ed.), *Fourteen steps in managing an aging workforce* (pp. 39–51). Lexington, MA: Lexington Books.

4. Blok, M. M., & de Looze, M. P. (2011). What is the evidence for less shift work tolerance in older workers? *Ergonomics, 54*, 221–232.

5. Sterns, H. L., Barrett, G. V., & Alexander, R. A. (1985). Accidents and the aging individual. In J. E. Birren & K.W. Schaie (Eds.), *Handbook of the psychology of aging* (pp. 703–724). New York, NY: Van Nostrand Reinhold.

6. Salthouse, T. (2012). Consequences of age-related cognitive declines. *Annual Review of Psychology, 63*, 201–226; Schaie, K. W. (1994). The course of adult intellectual development. *American Psychologist, 49*, 304–313.

7. Alessandri, G., Truxillo, D. M., Tisak, J., Fagnani, C., & Borgogni, L. (2020). Within-individual age-related trends, cycles, and event-driven changes in job performance: A career-span perspective. *Journal of Business and Psychology, 35*, 643–662.

8. Ng, T. W. H., & Feldman, D. C. (2008). The relationship of age to ten dimensions of job performance. *Journal of Applied Psychology, 93*, 392–423; Ng, T. W. H., & Feldman, D. C. (2010). The relationships of age with job attitudes: A meta-analysis. *Personnel Psychology, 63*, 677–718; Ng, T. W. H., & Feldman, D. C. (2013). Employee age and health. *Journal of Vocational Behavior, 83*, 336–345.

9. Salthouse, T. (2012). Consequences of age-related cognitive declines. *Annual Review of Psychology, 63*, 201–226.

10. Ackerman, P. L. (2017). Adult intelligence: The construct and the criterion problem. *Perspectives on Psychological Science, 12*(6), 987–998. https://doi.org/10.1177/1745691617703437; Inceoglu, I., Segers, J., & Bartram, D. (2012). Age-related differences in work motivation. *Journal of Occupational and Organizational Psychology, 85*, 300–329; Kooij, D. T., Kanfer, R., Betts, M., & Rudolph, C. W. (2018). Future time perspective: A systematic review and meta-analysis. *Journal of Applied Psychology, 103*, 867–893; Kooij, D. T. A. M., de Lange, A. H., Jansen, P. G. W., Kanfer, R., & Dikkers, J. S. E. (2011). Age and work-related motives: Results of a meta-analysis. *Journal of Organizational Behavior, 32*, 197–225; Roberts, B. W., Walton, K. E., & Viechtbauer, W. (2006). Patterns of mean-level change in personality traits across the life course: A meta-analysis of longitudinal studies. *Psychological Bulletin, 132*, 1–25; Salthouse, T. (2012); Soto, C. J., John, O. P., Gosling, S. D., & Potter, J. (2011). Age differences in personality traits from 10 to 65: Big five facets in a large cross-sectional sample. *Journal of Personality and Social Psychology, 100*, 330–348; Wille, B., Hofmans, J., Feys, M., & De Fruyt, F.

(2014). Maturation of work attitudes: Correlated change with Big Five personality traits and reciprocal effects over 15 years. *Journal of Organizational Behavior, 35*, 507–529.

11. Brady, G. M., Truxillo, D. M., Cadiz, D. M., Rineer, J. R., Caughlin, D. E., & Bodner, T. (2020). Opening the black box: Examining the nomological network of work ability and its role in organizational research. *Journal of Applied Psychology, 105*, 637–670; McGonagle, A. K., Fisher, G. G., Barnes-Farrell, J. L., & Grosch, J. W. (2015). Individual and work factors related to perceived work ability and labor force outcomes. *Journal of Applied Psychology, 100*, 376–398.

12. Brady et al (2020); Feldt, T., Hyvönen, K., Mäkikangas, A., Kinnunen, U., & Kokko, K. (2009). Development trajectories of Finnish managers' work ability over a 10-year follow-up period. *Scandinavian Journal of Work, Environment & Health, 35*, 37–47.

13. Ilmarinen, J., Tuomi, K., & Klockars, M. (1997). Changes in the work ability of active employees over an 11-year period. *Scandinavian Journal of Work, Environment & Health, 23*, 49–57.

14. Truxillo, D. M., Cadiz, D.M., & Brady, G. M. (2020). COVID-19 and its implications for research on work ability. *Work, Aging and Retirement, 6*, 242–245.

15. Robbins, J. M., Ford, M. T., & Tetrick, L. E. (2012). Perceived unfairness and employee health: A meta-analytic integration. *Journal of Applied Psychology, 97*, 235–272.

16. Brady, G. (2019). *Integrating work ability into the organizational science literature: Advancing theory and developing the nomological network* (Dissertation). Portland State University.

17. Loch, C., Sting, F., Bauer, N., & Mauermann, H. (2010). How BMW is defusing the demographic time bomb. *Harvard Business Review, 88*, 99–102.

18. *Total worker health in action!* Available at: https://www.cdc.gov/niosh/twh/newsletter/twhnewsv5n3.html

19. Teeple, E., Collins, J. E., Shrestha, S., Dennerlein, J. T., Losina, E., & Katz, J. N. (2017). Outcomes of safe patient handling and mobilization programs: A meta-analysis. *Work, 58*, 173–184.

20. Weigl, M., Müller, A., Hornung, S., Zacher, H., & Angerer, P. (2013). The moderating effects of job control and selection, optimization, and compensation strategies on the age–work ability relationship. *Journal of Organizational Behavior, 34*, 607–628.

21. Robbins et al (2012).

22. Boehm, S. A., Kunze, F., & Bruch, H. (2014). Spotlight on age-diversity climate: The impact of age-inclusive HR practices on firm-level outcomes. *Personnel Psychology, 67*, 667–704.

23. Bontrup, C., Taylor, W. R., Fliesser, M., Visscher, R., Green, T., Wippert, P. M., & Zemp, R. (2019). Low back pain and its relationship with sitting behaviour among sedentary office workers. *Applied Ergonomics, 81*, 102894.

Effective Teamwork and Relationships in Diverse Teams as Workers Evolve   **6**

Issues of diversity and inclusion in teams and relationships are increasingly in the forefront of the minds of managers and employees alike. That pair of words, *diversity and inclusion*, are heard often in today's workplace – but what exactly do they mean, why should they be fostered, and how can managers ensure they are doing all they can to support the true intention of these words? What's more, why are diversity and inclusion being highlighted in a book about the aging workforce?

This chapter takes a broad view of diversity, considering it both as a surface-level feature (like age, race, gender, etc.) and a deeper-level feature (like values, backgrounds, talents, etc.). We will focus much of this chapter on age diversity, highlighting the duality of age in this conversation about diversity – age in and of itself is a *feature of diversity*, and age *affects perceptions of other types of diversity*. Both of these ideas will be explored here. We will provide key current information regarding the benefits and challenges of diverse teams and of the relationships that develop among diverse team members. We will then focus on how people evolve over time in regard to their attitudes toward and management of diverse relationships given changes in their own age, experience, maturity, life-stage, and so forth.

We imagine most readers have already given some thought to ideas of diversity and inclusion. But perhaps they have not considered how these dynamics unfold over time as employees age, or as the diversity composition of a team develops. We will also provide some actionable steps, grounded in science-based inclusion practices and guided by our PIERA framework, so you can take the ideas that resonate with you and your work situation and do something with them. First, let's clarify the meanings of diversity and what we know about how it tends to play out at work.

Surface-Level and Deep-Level Diversity

Diversity, most simply, refers to differences among members of a workgroup. It seems the automatic association many people have with the term workplace "diversity" is race – that it means having people of different races working together. Although that is one important type of diversity, it is only one part of a much broader concept. And in fact, when we consider diversity very broadly, it doesn't just mean adding other demographics into the mix, like age or gender. It also means thinking about ways we differ on a deeper, and perhaps more work-relevant, level. This distinction recognizes that diversity can be surface-level (differences that we can see like ethnicity and gender) or deep-level (differences we may not see like personality and experiences that reflect more meaningful differences).

Surface-level diversity is sometimes called "bio-demographic diversity"[1] and reflects those differences that are visible to others. It is a very natural human tendency for us to categorize the people around us automatically, and so our minds likely register the race, gender, and at least approximate age of those we encounter at work. Then we decide if these features make those people the "same" or "different" from us. This doesn't mean that we necessarily dislike (feel prejudice toward) those who are different or treat them unfairly (discriminate) (although some people might and systems often do), but that we may have some automatic beliefs and expectations based on these features of others. We may assume that those who look like us *are* like us in some deeper ways (shared experiences and values, to name a couple), even if they are not. For example, the 30-something women on a team may assume that a new woman around their age who has joined the team is also a mother and sharing in the same struggles that they do, when in fact that is not part of the new teammate's life experience. In other words, we may assume that surface-level features signal meaningful differences between the individuals who display them, without actually getting to know those individuals to verify this assumption. At best, this can lead to surprises. At worst, it can lead to misunderstandings and conflict.

But people may be diverse at a deeper level, that is, in terms of their values, attitudes, interests, experiences, and talents.[2] Although these *deep-level traits* may correlate with some surface-level features to a small extent, they are by no means discoverable by "judging a book by its cover". All of these qualities come in vastly different packages. Someone who looks nothing like us may have a shared love of knitting, hip-hop, philosophy, and hockey, identify as a feminist, be high in introversion and agreeableness, and have a special talent for data visualization. Conversely, someone who shares our age, gender, and race may seem awfully similar to us on the surface but may actually have very little in common with us under the surface.

Deep-level diversity, in terms of our attitudes and skills for example, is more pertinent to our behavior at work than is surface-level diversity.[3] For example, more creative solutions to a problem will come from a group with different backgrounds and experiences than from one with only surface-level differences. That said, there are also important social justice reasons for insisting that people from historically disadvantaged groups have opportunities to make contributions across levels of the organization.

To add to this complexity, any particular work team may have one or two members who are dissimilar from everyone else. That is, the people on the team as a whole would be relatively similar to each other, but those few folks would be different from the others. Or a team may comprise quite a few people who have different surface-level and/or deep-level differences. Diversity issues are relevant to teams in both of these scenarios.

Benefits and Challenges of Diversity and Inclusion

The narrative about diversity has shifted; where it once was about "managing challenges" it is more often now about "leveraging benefits". It turns out that there may be both benefits and challenges to diverse teams – and in some cases, no effects at all. But whether diversity brings challenges or benefits likely depends on a host of factors.[4] The practice of inclusion, a newer way to broaden our thinking on diversity, can offer specific ideas to maximize the likelihood of beneficial outcomes.[5] Inclusion practices are behaviors that organizations, leaders, and members can take to foster voice, involvement, engagement, and authentic connections among all members. We will offer specific suggestions utilizing an inclusion perspective at the end of this chapter.

As mentioned above, one of the factors affecting the success of diverse teams is indeed whether the diversity stems from surface-level or deep-level differences. We mentioned that because surface-level characteristics are readily visible, they may immediately trigger feelings of sameness or differentness, and we are often naturally more comfortable at first with people similar to us. Discomfort around others who we think are different from us can lead to hyper-awareness about how we are coming across to others; trying to control our emotions and communication style can be awkward and distracting and take our attention away from the matters at hand. We might also make assumptions about others' experiences, skills, or attitudes that are based more on the demographic group attribute rather than what we know about the person. For example, someone might assume that the youngest person on the team is the whiz at new software, when actually an older member of the team is the most knowledgeable in this area. This can lead to miscommunications, and might even cause offence, and hinder team cohesion.

There is some good news in relation to these potential drawbacks of demographic diversity. First of all, they tend to diminish over time as group members interact and get to know each other.[6] Demographic differences also don't tend to be as prominent if the differences aren't also associated with status differences in the workplace.[7] And, if the organization (or at least the immediate work context, like the department or store) has strong values for inclusiveness of all employees, demographic differences may not affect the closeness and interactions of the group members. There are some things that can be done to enhance these factors – we'll get to these soon. But first, let's look at some of the potential outcomes of teams where deep-level differences exist.

Deep-level differences are interesting because of the many ways that team members differ. Some of these differences may be a matter of attitudes – what team members feel about the organization and its practices, whether they like their job, or even their political leanings. Some of these may be related to even more deep-seated values and life principles. Still others may be most clearly related to the mission and charge of the team – that is, differences in experiences, skills, talents, and knowledge.

The common wisdom has long been that deep-level diversity should enhance teams. The thinking is that each unique perspective that is brought to the group should broaden its ability to make wise decisions, overcome challenges, and thereby yield a higher level of productivity (both in terms of quantity and quality). And, indeed, there is some evidence of these positive effects, especially for complicated tasks and those requiring some creativity and innovation. If you consider some of those deep-level differences described above, however, you can probably see how deep-level differences also have the power to impede the processes that lead to a high level of team performance.[8] For example, the dislike and even avoidance that may come from interacting with a person with whom you butt heads on matters of world politics or trust in the organization may make it difficult to see the helpful perspective that person would bring to the team. Even if there aren't any outright disagreements or even acknowledgment of diversity in values, that doesn't mean that the job-related differences in experience and skills that each member brings will be effectively integrated to solve the task at hand.

Of course, life is messy, and it is quite likely that teams have a variety of surface- and deep-level differences – differences that become visible at different times in the course of the team's work. Some of these differences, as we mentioned, may fade with time. But others could intensify or return (for better or worse) depending on the current focus of the team's work, current affairs of the organization, or even the larger environment in which the organization is embedded.

This awareness is important for all types of managers, team leaders, and team members, but for the purposes of this book we want to put an even more specific lens on this discussion: *What role do age differences and the aging process play in best practices for managing and capitalizing on a diverse workforce?*

Age as a Type of Diversity

We have said that age is one characteristic by which team members may differ. Age is typically classified as a "surface-level" diversity characteristic – part of what we see right way – though like other things in that category it is often believed to be associated with other more meaningful characteristics. Some of these may be based purely on generalizations, and sometimes age may signal real developmental differences among people. Some of these differences could interfere with team functioning, and some of them could enhance it. For example, perhaps in one age-diverse marketing team younger members believe older members think they are too inexperienced and won't listen to them, so they hold back sharing a potentially innovative idea. Meanwhile, in a rival company's marketing team, it is clear to members of all ages that their perspectives will be given fair consideration and valued in part *because* of the unique vantage point that their past and current life experiences bring to bear.

There are a multitude of stereotypes that bubble to the surface when we note a person's age. Stereotypes don't only apply to older workers; we make generalizations about the characteristics of younger and middle-aged workers as well.[9] Even if we are the type of people who try hard not to stereotype others, stereotypes are pervasive in our culture and accentuated by the media we consume daily. Not only that, stereotypes are ways that our brain creates shortcuts – creating categories (e.g., in my group/in another group) for all the people we encounter is a natural way for us to process information to get us through the day. Thus, it is virtually impossible not to be affected by them. Negative stereotypes of older workers include being slow, grouchy, set in their ways, resistant to change, conservative, and technologically incompetent. Negative stereotypes of younger workers include being entitled, narcissistic, lazy, naïve or inexperienced, and having a low attention span. We also have expectations about the positive characteristics of these age groups – older workers are thought to be experienced and loyal, for example, and younger workers are thought to be energetic and creative. Although positive stereotypes may seem less harmful on their face, making any assumption or expectation about a person solely based on their age category is unfair and often inaccurate.

Science has provided some evidence that age diversity in teams can sometimes interfere with how close the members of a team feel, how much they share technical information, and how they express (or suppress) their emotions on teams.[10] This does not necessarily mean that these things will happen with the age-diverse teams in your organization. Or it may be that it will only happen under certain specific circumstances.

For example, if resources are tight in an organization, or if younger people feel as if their upward mobility in the organization is limited because older people are not leaving the organization at the rate they once did, this could cause some negative feelings between age groups. By the same token, if older people believe those younger than them are gunning for their jobs, they may have a harder time building trust with those team members. Overall, the economic situation in the organization and in the larger context may trickle down to impact team functioning on age-diverse teams.

Cultural issues may also play a role. It's been suggested, for example, that in cultures where there is a lot of social distance and stratification among people from different status groups – and where status is conferred at least in part by aging – there could be more respect shown to older people by younger people. But there may also be less open and honest communication.[11] Cultures that value collectivism – the good of the group over the individual – may find less discord among age-diverse groups.

Aside from the role of the environment, like economics and culture, there are also some other differences between people besides their age that might impact how they react in age-diverse teams. For example, to the degree that some people are scared of their own aging, the end of their career, and even the inevitable end of life, the more they might want to avoid older people because it is a reminder of these future events in their own lives.[12]

Our age is likely not the only way we differ on the surface from others on our teams – we may be mixed in terms of race, gender, and other visible features. Age beliefs and expectations may be different, for example, for an older woman as compared with an older man. And, if these differences on a team cluster in any way – for example, if most of the younger people are women and the older people are men, the divisions among team members (literally called "faultlines" in the research in this area, like in geology) may be more challenging (but not impossible!) to cross.[13]

Stating that age is a surface-level characteristic does not mean that there may not be systematic, meaningful, or perhaps helpful differences among team members that are in part due to their age. As we've been emphasizing throughout the book, aging can be associated with different life experiences, work experiences, and preferences – it just doesn't automatically come in lock step with those things. Some of our skills and abilities improve over time with practice and expertise, while others diminish over time with physical and mental decline. Notably, the rates of changes across people vary quite a bit.

One particularly pertinent question is whether people's acceptance and appreciation of diversity (of all kinds), or stated on the flip side, whether people's level of prejudice against members of diverse groups, changes systematically with age. Additionally, we can also consider whether the way an employee works in teams may change as they age. We tackle these questions next.

Approaches to Diversity and Teamwork over the Lifespan

In the prior section we talked about some of the stereotypes we have about people based on their age group. A common belief about older people is that they are closed-minded and set in their ways. This sounds like a recipe for disaster when introducing diversity into an organization or a team. On the flip side, a common positive belief about younger people is that they are open-minded, welcoming of change, and accepting of difference. Is this true? Will it be the young people who embrace and champion diversity and the older people who, at best, will begrudgingly come to accept the new reality?

Not necessarily – it is not that cut and dried. Sadly, one can find many examples in the news of young people spewing hateful messages about people different from them. One can also find examples of older adults demonstrating for fair treatment for all. It is impossible to know any one person's attitude toward diversity by checking the age on their driver's license.

Having said that, there is recent research evidence that shows that *on average* acceptance of diversity is more common among younger people than among older people, and that rates of reported prejudiced attitudes (and more implicit negative attitudes as well) are more common among older people than younger. Why is that?

The most common explanation is that times have changed; older people came of age at a time when people from different ethnic groups were less integrated, when women had fewer rights and were in less prominent positions in the workforce, and when LGBTQ people were less likely to be open about their identities. Although that is true – times have changed – it is unlikely to fully explain differences between age groups. Older people, especially those still employed, are often currently exposed to the same diversity information and resources as younger people.

Some interesting neuroscience explanations have emerged that indicate that perhaps it isn't just a difference between generations, such that diversity has become more acceptable in modern times, that is producing this gap in the acceptance of diversity. Rather, it may be at least in part that subtle changes in our brains may make it more difficult to inhibit stereotypic thoughts at older ages.[14,15] As we age, changes in the part of the brain (prefrontal cortex) – that help us inhibit the odd bits of information that pop into our minds until we've sorted out what is actually useful and accurate – starts to decline. The scientists are quick to point out that this finding absolutely doesn't mean that older people are likely to be prejudiced against those who are different; just that younger brains are more efficient in keeping such automatic judgments in check before they can be evaluated. People differ vastly in their degree of prejudice (dislike or even hate of those who belong to different groups), but even very open-minded people from all groups are exposed to information that could trigger a stereotype. As we age it may become more difficult to recognize information that in the past we could easily dismiss and deem irrelevant to our interactions. Although this research finding is new, there are a number of important questions that must be answered to understand the boundaries of this effect. For example, at what age is this effect more likely to kick in (the "older people" in this early research average in the 80s, older than most workers)? And, what can be done to help prevent the effects of this decline? In the meanwhile, if you've known someone for decades and it seems they are sometimes expressing attitudes you wouldn't expect from them, this could in part explain what's going on.

On the other hand, when teams have worked together over periods of time, those surface differences that at first might have disrupted communication and work efficiency may fade to the background, and the deep-level similarities and differences among team members are more likely to have an impact on team functioning.[16] The members of long-standing teams come to know each other's work styles, preferences, talents, and weaknesses – and they know what pushes each other's buttons. People are not static, though, and members of long-standing teams progress through different life stages – highs and lows – that could affect the dynamics of the team over time.

For example, people's interest in teamwork in terms of what they gain from it and what aspects of it they prefer may change over time. Often at the start of a career employees are eager to learn all they can, demonstrate their skills, get experiences they can capitalize on, and build relationships that allow for career networking opportunities. But over time, people often change these goals. Later in a career, they may be drawn to team-work as a chance to contribute something unique to the team based on their vast experiences, build closer relationships with those they already know, and have the opportunity to teach others and pass on wisdom.[17] Note that "start of career" and "later in career" does not go hand in hand for everyone with age. People who switch careers at a later age may be motivated more similarly to other new people rather than those in their age group who have been at it for some time.

Applying the Concepts: How to Harness Age Diversity in Teams

Up until now in this chapter, we have discussed the potential pros and cons of diverse teams. We have also noted how diversity can have different effects both across the lifespan of the team itself as well as across the lifespan of team members. In this section we provide some guidance into how managers and team leaders (and team members themselves) can enhance the likelihood of benefiting from diverse teams, and how age and lifespan can be considered in these strategies. We will conclude with some advice on developing a PIERA plan, and we will provide examples of action steps you can take right now, in the next week, and in the long term.

Enhancing the Benefits of Diverse Teams Across the Lifespan: An Inclusion Approach

There is an array of options to consider if a diverse team appears to be functioning at a sub-optimal level. In considering what approach to take, a critical first step is to decide if what is needed is a general team building intervention or an intervention that specifically targets diversity? It could be that a team is struggling for reasons that have little or nothing to do with the surface- or deep-level differences among its members. Assuming diversity is the issue without investigating more closely could lead to choosing the wrong solution. Taking a PIERA approach and spending time on the planning stage will be worth it.

Although there is no shortage of case studies that sing the praises of team-building activities, they are also sometimes accompanied by some eye rolling on the part of participants. Do they work? The science indicates that they are not a panacea for all team problems. But on average some benefits do seem to result from team-building activities that are designed for these purposes: setting goals, improving interpersonal processes, clarifying roles, and solving problems.[18] Setting goals and clarifying roles seem to have the strongest effects, often resulting in improved attitudes and team process functioning. Sometimes hardline performance or productivity improvements can result as well. If your initial investigation points to the idea that your team(s) could benefit from general team building, a list of specific resources is available in Special Focus Box 6.1.

If you believe that diversity specifically needs to be targeted as a direct subject of an intervention, there are many approaches here as well. The current science suggests that incorporating inclusive practices are foundational for enhancing the likelihood that diversity can produce benefits. Inclusionary practices tend to be universally appealing – the need to belong and to be seen as a unique person are part of the human experience – but they may especially benefit those who have not historically felt comfortable, safe, and heard.[19] Moreover, by enhancing the inclusion climate in a team (or, if we are thinking big, in an organization), other types of interventions may be facilitated. That's because people will be less cynical about their purpose and more likely to be real and valuable contributors in

---

Special Focus Box 6.1: Team Building Resources

Dutton, J. E. (2003). *Energize your workplace: How to create and sustain high-quality connections at work.* San Francisco: Jossey-Bass.

Ferdman, B. M., & Deane, B. R. (2014). *Diversity at work: The practice of inclusion.* San Francisco: Jossey-Bass.

Lee, B. (2017). *Trust rules: How the world's best managers create great places to work.* Dublin, Ireland: Trust Lab Press.

Miller, B. (2015). *Quick team building activities for busy managers: 50 exercises that get results in 15 minutes.* New York: AMACOM.

Ozenk, K. & Hagan, M. (2019). *Rituals for work: 50 ways to create engagement, shared purpose, and a culture that can adapt to change.* Hoboken, NJ: Wiley.

Perry, R. (2018) *Belonging at work: Everyday interactions you can take to cultivate an inclusive organization.* Portland, OR: RPC Academy Press.

Robins, S. L. (2018). *What if? Short stories to spark inclusion and diversity dialogue.* Boston, MA: Nicholas Breely Publishing.

---

the process.[20] Diversity initiatives that are perceived as a "band-aid" to help avoid lawsuits or to merely tick a check box can make things worse.

To understand specifically how to bring the experience of inclusivity to a team it helps to get a clearer sense of what it means to have an experience of inclusion. When a person feels included, they feel safe (psychologically and physically), known and valued for their authentic self, respected, liked, and heard. This last point is crucial as there is a difference between being given a voice that later has no real influence and given a true opportunity to foster change.

Research in various companies has uncovered some of the actual behaviors that team members and leaders can perform regularly to promote an inclusive experience.[21] However, we echo others in suggesting that ideas for what will work in YOUR organization be collected locally, and in doing so – by asking and listening to everyone – you already have one step on the path to promoting inclusivity. We have some suggestions for how to do that in Special Focus Box 6.2.

That said, some common suggestions from promoting inclusivity include showing curiosity about others' experiences, really listening to and authentically sharing stories of personal experiences, and making sure everyone who wants to share information has equal opportunity and "floor time" for doing so. Leaders have a special responsibility in the team to serve as a role model of authenticity (do your team members really know you as a human?) and transparency (does everyone really understand why

Special Focus Box 6.2: Questions for Generating Team-Relevant Inclusive Behaviors

Industrial-Organizational psychologist Bernardo M. Ferdman has created a set of questions to provide to your team to get them thinking about ways that they can work together to co-create more inclusion in the team. These questions can be used verbatim or adapted or expanded to fit your team. It may be helpful to allow people to think about these questions individually and then share their answers in whatever venue you think would be most comfortable. For example, they could submit to the team leader, who would share answers anonymously to the group for discussion, or they could be shared verbally in a meeting where rules of trust and safety have been established.

1. What does the term inclusion mean?
2. What behaviors – from you or from others – help *you* feel more inclusion?
3. What behaviors help *others* around you feel more inclusion?
4. Imagine that you waved a magic wand and suddenly everyone in the world behaves inclusively, in a way that brings inclusion to life in every encounter with others. What *inclusive behaviors* do you see around you?
5. Imagine the most inclusive organization in the world, one in which everyone's talents, beliefs, backgrounds, capabilities, and ways of living – their uniqueness – is engaged, valued, and leveraged. What are on or two vital *inclusive organization policies and practices* in that organization?

things unfold as they do?).[22] Some team members may resist disclosure of personal information, and this should be respected, and reasons for resistance should be revisited over time to ensure that it isn't due to team or leader behaviors that are fixable. Leaders should include the whole team in setting team communication norms and expectations. Leaders should also regularly interact with members to get a sense of their own inclusion experiences and how they can be improved. Some teams may be entirely virtual, some may have virtual members, and some may interact at least part time on a virtual basis. Clearly, the COVID-19 pandemic led to this being a more widespread practice, and there has been much speculation that virtual interaction will become more normative as a result. Nurturing inclusion in these environments has its own challenges as there are fewer opportunities to interact casually, and communication can be more easily misinterpreted in this medium. Encouraging virtual teams to take the time to get to know each member fully and even to spend time in "virtual" coffee breaks or happy hours can help with this.[23]

Although these suggestions sound clear and simple, the path to change will always have some roadblocks. Some people may have to become a little more uncomfortable before everyone can become comfortable. For example, some people might find diversity-related conversations awkward, or worry about saying something by accident that is offensive to others. Having this expectation may prevent the team from giving up on these types of changes prematurely. Also, inclusion is often misinterpreted as meaning that everyone cooperates and agrees all the time and never debates issues. Such an approach can stifle real change and genuine belonging. If no ideas are ever challenged, decision-making and actual action on a task could be near impossible. An open conversation about what inclusion is and isn't may help quash myths and overcome concerns about change.

Inclusion practices are not short-term solutions to a problem, but new ways of being at work that will be ongoing and evolving. The specific behaviors may need to change over time with the addition of new members with new experiences, and as veteran members evolve in their lives and work. Moving toward increased inclusion is a great way, and possibly a necessary way, to intervene to enhance the benefits of diversity.

Other Approaches

There are specific issues that can be addressed with additional practices. For example, interpersonal biases stemming from stereotypes of other groups can lead people to feel discomfort around team members when issues relevant to those stereotypes bubble up. Let's say a team is called upon to get up to speed quickly on a new software system – younger team members may fear older team members won't be able to keep up and will bring the team down, and older team members may feel extra scrutiny and pressure because they sense these judgments. A team leader or manager can keep an eye out for changes in team demands that could trigger stereotypes about the subgroups within a team. Sharing this observation and inviting members to reflect on these stereotypes in a constructive fashion in a safe space without fear of scrutiny or retribution, can bring this into the open – with everyone feeling that they are on the same team.

If it seems that people from different backgrounds are having trouble connecting, initiatives to find common ground can be useful. It is important to do this, though, from the perspective of inclusivity. *The goal is not to try to make real differences among people invisible; rather, it is to look for the common bond among team members even while appreciating and valuing those differences.* All team members have multiple identities – some obvious, some not – but one that they all share is that they are all team members! As team members (and thus by definition shared organization members as well) they can derive a shared positive identity from these associations. Team members can be reminded that that connection can become a more positive source of overall pride the more that each team member contributes to the shared good of the team.

In addition to the shared connection of the team, there are likely many other commonalities that members share – if not all members, then perhaps pairs or small groups of members who on the surface look like they would be unlikely to have things in common. Building the opportunity for human connection into team meetings can help members uncover these shared passions, habits, and experiences. Ultimately this can reduce a sense of "us" and "them" and help to develop a stronger sense of "we".

All of these pursuits will be more natural to the extent that the organization has already made genuine efforts toward inclusivity and/or exhibits characteristics of a learning organization. Even if it is not the case, though, small efforts at the more local level of the team and department can have a ripple effect and should not be dismissed as not worth the work. It's the right thing to do. Certainly, though, if a manager feels ill-equipped for handling diversity dilemmas within their team it would be wise to speak to their own supervisors and consider utilizing the services of a trained diversity consultant.

The PIERA Approach to an Age Inclusion Team Intervention

We encourage you to reflect on the ideas in this chapter in light of your own teams and use the PIERA structure to test out a small-scale change toward helping your diverse teams flourish. In this section we walk you through an example of what this would look like, but as always you are encouraged to only take on something that makes sense for you and your organization.

Planning

- Are there teams that you manage or that you are a part of that are diverse in some way and that could be more effective and more cohesive?
- On what surface-level dimensions is the team diverse? On what deep-level dimensions is the team diverse?
- To what degree do you suspect that issues on the team are related to specifically to diversity? How can you find that out?
- Does each member of your team feel truly included and valued as an equal, respected, and liked contributor?

- Does your organization and/or your supervisor encourage you to promote inclusivity on your team? Would you need to get buy-in or permission to pursue a systematic change in this area?

You may be able to answer some of these questions on your own, but some may require further inquiry to your team members and superiors. You may consider both individual conversations and an initial feeler conversation with the team to gauge reactions. Or, another systematic approach would be to pair up younger team members with older team members and ask them to discuss what age-relevant issues they see on the team. Another option would be a confidential survey.

Once your data are gathered and reviewed, do you have a better sense of what might be driving the issue you were seeing? List out very <u>clear and specific objectives</u> for your pilot intervention.

Implementation

For the sake of this example, we are walking you through one specific small-scale intervention to help increase age inclusivity on your team. What this looks like for you may differ, depending on the results of the planning stage.

The objectives of the age inclusivity intervention are to:

- Have team members generate and share what age inclusivity would feel like to them.
- Have team members generate and share examples of specific behaviors that they and you as a leader can start doing to work toward a shared experience of age inclusivity on the team.
- Have team members generate and share a list of challenges that could arise to disrupt this process, and to also generate and share some potential solutions to those challenges.

Prior to the start of this program, a short bulleted list of reasons why this is being tested out should be provided to the team, and dates will be scheduled for a series of meetings where these activities will take place. The meetings should have a specific start and stop time that will be respected and should have a clear agenda. Ground rules for communication (based on principles of inclusivity) should be provided and emphasized. Depending on the size of the team, it may be divided into smaller teams so that it will be easier for everyone to be able to contribute. Procedures will be put in place to evaluate the approach midstream to decide if it needs adjustment.

Having some structured activities and discussions will improve the likelihood that members can stay focused on the issue and allow them to focus on changing behaviors and not finger-pointing. For example, perhaps they can work (in small groups, if the team is large) on describing in detail what a completely age-inclusive team would look like and one that was not at all inclusive. Members can write down examples of specific behaviors that made them feel included or excluded, based on their age, in the last month and those can be shared anonymously by the team leader as examples. Members can also write down examples of age stereotypes that they believe are sometimes held about their group, and the whole group (all ages) can think about ways they could be overcome.

The team members and the leader will leave the last meeting with a specific list of agreed-upon behaviors to try out over the course of the next month. The leader will remind everyone of the plan to try them briefly at the start of meetings, and at least once a week via a short and friendly email reminder. The leader will be available for consultation on how to execute behaviors or any concerns of any team member.

Evaluation

Soon after the sessions have ended, reactions to them can be assessed with a brief, anonymous electronic survey (or, if not technically feasible, paper-and-pencil surveys with a drop-box). Questions can be directed at the perceived usefulness of the sessions. Finally, after the month trial period of behaviors has ended, a final survey can look at the perceived usefulness of the trial, gauge whether each objective is perceived to have been accomplished, and importantly, whether issues of age inclusivity remain. Open-ended questions can ask for suggestions on how to tackle the issue going forward.

Reflection

Prior to compiling the data the team leader should reflect on their own about their perception of how they believed things changed over the course of the month. Did any palpable change occur? Was it consistent over the month, or did it die down after a honeymoon period? Did unexpected things happen?

Once the data are compiled, the leader should look for trends. Do the data mirror the leader' own reflections? Where are there inconsistencies? Is anything jumping out as particularly successful or unsuccessful?

Following a private reflection and notes, the data can be shared with the team in a digestible format. What are their reactions? An open discussion period should be scheduled once they have a chance to reflect carefully. Also, the leader should be available for private discussions as well.

As we noted earlier, if a leader is uncomfortable with handling this (or any stage) of this type of intervention on their own, they may want to ask HR for a coach. For example, at this stage a trained facilitator could show that there is organizational support for this activity and provide a second set of ears and eyes to help gauge reactions of the various team members during the feedback session.

Adjustment

Based on the reflection period, a meeting can be scheduled to take suggestions for adjusting team policy and practices regarding inclusion based on interpretation of its level of success. It is ill advised to give up on the idea of age inclusion if the results were disappointing. How can it be approached in a different manner?

If there was more success than failure, how can this pilot be used to implement more permanent changes? Are their lessons learned in this team that could inform other teams or other levels of the organization?

Action Items: Things to Do Right Now, Next Week, and Long Term

Things to Do Right Now

Get out a piece of paper or open a blank computer file. Imagine that next year at this time everyone on your team expresses having the experience of feeling completely included on the team. What are ways you imagine them describing that experience?

Things to Do Next Week

Take a look at the list of behaviors that are often thought to foster inclusion. Pick three to try out next week. Take the description of the behavior as it appears and turn it into a very specific behavior that you can do with your team that makes sense in your context. For example, is there a volunteer activity age-diverse team members can work on together – say, an afternoon at a food bank? At the end of the week, take 10–15 minutes to reflect on how this went.

Things to Do Long Term

Take some time to investigate your organization's Diversity & Inclusion history and current policies. Do they include age as a relevant category? If not, can its inclusion in these policies be championed? Are there people on the team who would want to work with you on that? If so, do they reflect simplistic generational thinking, or do they acknowledge individual variability in life experiences and timelines? Can they be improved?

Notes

1. Horwitz, S. K., & Horwitz, I. B. (2007). The effects of team diversity on team outcomes: A meta-analytic review of team demography. *Journal of Management, 33*, 987–1015.
2. Harrison, D. A., Price, K. H., & Bell, M. P. (1998). Beyond relational demography: Time and the effects of surface- and deep-level diversity on work group cohesion. *Academy of Management Journal, 41*, 96–107.
3. van Dijk, H., van Engan, M. L., & van Knippenberg, D. (2012). Defying conventional wisdom: A meta-analytical investigation of the differences between demographic and job-related diversity relationships with performance. *Organizational Behavior and Human Decision Processes, 119*, 38–53.
4. Roberson, Q., Ryan, A. M., & Ragins, B. R. (2017). The evolution and future of diversity at work. *Journal of Applied Psychology, 1–2*, 483–499.
5. Ferdman, B. M. (2014). The practice of inclusion in diverse organizations. In B. M. Ferdman & B. R. Deane (Eds.), *Diversity at work: The practice of inclusion* (pp. 3–54). San Francisco, CA: Jossey-Bass.
6. Harrison et al. (1998).
7. Roberson, Q. M. (2019). Diversity in the workplace: A review, synthesis, and future research agenda. *Annual Review of Organizational Psychology and Organizational Behavior, 6*, 69–88.
8. Ibid.
9. Finkelstein, L. M., Ryan, K. M., & King, E. B. (2013). What do the young (old) people think of me? Content and accuracy of age-based metastereotypes. *European Journal of Work and Organizational Psychology, 22*, 633–657.
10. Imose, R. A., & Finkelstein, L. M. (2018). A multilevel theoretical framework integrating diversity and emotional labor. *Group and Organizational Management, 43*, 718–751.
11. Perry, E. L., & Parlamis, J. D. (2006). Age and ageism in organizations: A review and consideration of national culture. In A. M. Konrad, P. Prasad, & J. K. Pringle (Eds.), *Handbook of workplace diversity* (pp. 345–370). New York, NY: Sage Publications.
12. Martens, A., Goldenberg, J. L., & Greenberg, J. (2005). A terror management perspective on ageism. *Journal of Social Issues, 61*, 223–239.
13. Kunze, F., & Boehm, S. (2015). Age diversity and global teamwork: A future agenda for researchers and practitioners. In L. M. Finkelstein, D. M. Truxillo, F. Fraccaroli, & R. Kanfer (Eds.), *Facing the challenges of a multi-age workforce: A use-inspired approach* (pp. 27–49). New York: Routledge.

14. von Hippel, W., Silver, L. A., & Lynch, M. E. (2000). Stereotyping against your will: The role of inhibitory ability in stereotyping and prejudice among the elderly. *Personality and Social Psychology Bulletin, 26,* 523–532.

15. Gonsalkorale, K., Sherman, J. W., Klauer, K C. (2009). Aging and prejudice: Diminished regulation of automatic race bias among older adults. *Journal of Experimental Social Psychology, 45,* 410–414.

16. Harrison, D. A., Price, K. H., Gavin, J. H., & Florey, A. T. (2002). Time, teams, and task performance: Changing effects of surface- and deep-level diversity on group functioning. *Academy of Management Journal, 45,* 1029–1045.

17. Gartner, L. U. A., & Hertel, G. (2017). Future time perspective in occupational teams: Do older workers prefer more familiar teams? *Frontiers in Psychology, 8,* 1613–1639.

18. Klein, C. DiazGranados, D., Salas, E., Le, H., Burke, C. S., Lyons, R. Goodwin, G. F. (2009). Does team building work? *Small Group Research, 40,* 181–222.

19. Ferdman (2014).

20. Pless, N. M., & Maak, T. (2004). Building an inclusive diversity culture: Principles, processes and practice. *Journal of Business Ethics, 54,* 129–147.

21. Ferdman (2014).

22. Pless and Maak (2004).

23. Holton, J. A. (2001). Building trust and collaboration in a virtual team. *Team Performance Management: An International Journal, 7,* 36–47.

Enhancing Work-Nonwork Balance and Well-Being of Evolving Workers

7

What Is Work-Life Balance?

This chapter is devoted to work-nonwork balance as we age. In Chapter 2, you already had a short introduction to this topic and its relevance with regard to the quality of individual and organizational life. Work-nonwork balance goes by many names: *work-life balance*; *work-nonwork balance*; *work-family balance*. Others use the term *"conflict"*, instead of balance, to describe the negative side of the relationship between work roles and domains outside of work, such as family context, leisure time, and the community where a person lives. Yet others talk about "work-life integration" or "work-life alignment". The central point is to understand how your work relates to, interacts with, can interfere with, and may even enhance other areas of your life – and vice-versa. In this chapter we chose to use the label *"work-nonwork life balance"*.

Consider this example. Imagine Robert, a middle-aged man (45 years old) who works as an advanced laboratory technician for a large pharmaceutical company. As part of his job, he is responsible for coordinating the activities of 12 coworkers who also work with very sophisticated biomedical analysis tools, but nine of whom work a different shift. The task sheets provided to workers are often incomplete, and because of his role as a coordinator, Robert is often called at home by his colleagues to help decipher task sheets. Although Robert is passionate about his work and is committed to the company, work calls on his evenings and often interrupts family time and activities with his two children and wife, Sarah, who is employed as a school manager in the same city. Sarah's job also involves a lot of responsibility, but it does not usually require her to be available when she is not at work. Robert is very keen on being with his children and participating in the significant events of their growth. Although the distribution of family obligations between Robert and Sarah is equitable and career development is important to both partners, their job demands typically require substantial negotiation of priorities that sometimes leads to conflict between them. For example, a new responsibility for Sarah in a challenging project for her school may require Robert's presence in the family to cover some childcare loads. Robert and Sarah also enjoy a number of sports and community activities, such as sailing and cheering on the local basketball team, and they look forward to engaging in activities with their young children on weekends. And as part of a larger religious community, they are committed to following the rituals of their community and to cultivating their children's spiritual growth.

As this example shows, our work activities do not exist in a vacuum, but are intertwined in the rich fabric of life activities that include both passions and obligations to family, friends, community, leisure, and spiritual well-being. Each person seeks a balance between the different roles played in different areas of life. These areas are usually divided into "domains" that have varying levels of priority depending on interests, values, and obligations. The "boundaries" between these domains can, in turn, be understood as either inviolable (nothing can interfere with a certain area of life) or flexible (some interferences can be tolerated without serious consequences). Possible conflicts can result when the pressure from different domains are incompatible in some way, such as if a sudden evening phone call from the workplace interrupts a family dinner with friends or if the commitment of a business trip forces the person to give up an important sporting event with their children. These examples are related to a work interference in the family life (WIF). Other possible conflicts occur when family impediments, for example, the illness of a child or moving to a new home, hinder the performance of work obligations (FIW). In these cases, the different roles played by a person come into conflict, and the balance between work and the nonwork domains can be upended.

Having clarified what is meant by balance between work and nonwork life, now try to do these simple mental exercises:

a. Think of the same worker profile described above, but *reverse* Robert and Sarah's work roles. In your opinion, what is the probability that work-related interruptions by Sarah's coworkers will lead to higher levels of conflict in Sarah's life? And if so, why?

b. Think about Robert's situation 15 years down the road, when he is 60 and his children are about 20 years old. In your opinion, what is the likelihood that he continues to experience the same amount of work-nonwork conflict? More or less? In which direction?

c. What could Robert's company do to reduce the potential work-nonwork conflict? Which interventions could be applied? And with what advantages and risks?

Most likely you came to the conclusion that there is a gender asymmetry in the management of work-nonwork life balance between life domains, to the disadvantage of women. As for point (b), you probably thought about how changing life circumstances as we get older might reduce the likelihood of conflict – although this is not always the case. And for point (c), the answer is yes, but a structured methodology is needed – and *PIERA* can help us in this task.

The Psychological Relevance of a Work-Nonwork Life Balance

From an individual's point of view, the balance between *work and nonwork* life depends on numerous psychological characteristics. Maintaining a balance between areas of life means making choices in everyday life (how much of my time do I spend at work at the expense of my family). It also means making long-term strategic decisions (I move away from my hometown for a new job position; I give up a job promotion because it would require too much time commitment). These choices and decisions are influenced by basic elements of our personality (what type of person I am?) and our self-concept and identity (what are my values and aspirations? What is the ideal image I have of myself?). See Special Focus Box 7.1.

That is, achieving balance is more than a rational or logistical task, but rather a *psychological* task that each of us carries out continuously across our lifespan. It is also a task that shapes, and is shaped by, our evolving identity and self-concept as we age. Throughout our lives we make choices – to postpone the leisure time activities, to reach agreement (e.g., accepting a career sacrifice to allow your partner to develop their career), or to abdicate some moral principle (e.g., work during religious holidays)

Special Focus Box 7.1: Career Choices and Lifestyle

Edgar Schein, a well-known organizational psychologist, believes that career choices are guided by some career anchors that each of us possesses and "activates" when we make important decisions in planning our career. Following the Schein definition, career anchors include talents, motives, values, and attitudes that give stability and direction to a person's career. A career anchor is an element in the self-concept that will not give up, even in the face of difficult choices.

One of the possible anchors is related to "lifestyle":

"Those who are focused first on lifestyle look at their whole pattern of living. Rather than balance work and life, they are more likely to integrate the two. They may even take long periods of time off work in which to indulge in passions such as travelling".

If you are interested to know which is your career anchors, please have a look at this website: https://rapidbi.com/careeranchors/

that are driven by the demands of our various roles and that can alter our sense of identity. Exercising different roles that are in conflict with each other leads to resource drain (mental and emotional resources). This drain can have both short- and long-term negative effects on physical health and/or psychological well-being. Many studies[1] have shown that the work-nonwork imbalance and interference is associated with lower life satisfaction (to be more specific, with less work, career, and marital satisfaction). In extreme cases a lack of balance between life domains can engender psychological strain, somatic symptoms, and substance abuse. Work-nonwork imbalance is also considered a determinant of burnout syndrome, a state of exhaustion and cynicism about the value of one's occupation. At the same time, strain and burnout could be considered antecedents of work-family conflict. This highlights the possible vicious circle between imbalances in the areas of life and individual distress.[2]

From a personal point of view, the balance between different life domains is a matter of perception. A person can perceive a balance between work and nonwork activity when s/he is able to navigate between the different social roles (being a worker with responsibilities; being a good father/mother; being a devoted believer; etc.) without strong conflicts within themselves or with others.

Research also defines some psychological processes that affect the balance between work and nonwork.

- *Time management*: being able to prevent conflicts between requests coming from different domains, for example, through a strong capacity for time management and a clear definition of priorities (e.g., what is important for myself?);
- *Segmentation*: being able to clearly define the boundaries between work and other life activities and actively regulating the strength of these boundaries. This could mean reducing the opportunities for different life domains to interfere with each other (e.g., not responding to e-mail during the time dedicated to the family);
- *Prevention*: anticipating and preventing the possible conflicts that can occur because of interferences between different spheres of life. For example, one could "negotiate" with family the possible invasion of the working sphere if the job requires it.

It is important to recognize that successfully managing these processes has considerable advantages. If the interferences among areas of life are well-regulated by the individual and their family, then a person may enjoy the benefits, including improved well-being. This might require being able to discuss some work problems in the family and get help and support from them, or finding the opportunity to cultivate interests and hobbies with some colleagues in the workplace. The work experience can benefit from a good family climate as well; that is, the work experience can become a resource for other life domains. We will discuss how to better manage these boundaries between work and nonwork and their implications for different life stages.

Work-Life Balance as a Societal Issue

The theme of work-life balance cannot be reduced to the individual and psychological levels only. It is so important to a healthy citizenry that national, international, and state institutions address the issue. A single example, taken from a volume by the philosopher Martha C. Nussbaum,[3] clarifies this point. In the 1950s, a textile worker from South Carolina was required (for organizational reasons) to work on Saturdays. Her religious beliefs prevented her from working on Saturdays. Not being able to enforce this right of conscience by her work organization, she was forced to resign. Following her difficulties in obtaining unemployment benefits, she appealed to the Court. The US Supreme Court decided in favor of the worker (1963; https://supreme.justia.com/cases/federal/us/374/398/). This case shows that values and principles of conscience are sometimes legally stronger than organizational constraints and existing laws for access to unemployment benefits. It also shows how the balance between the work and nonwork spheres can be protected by institutions.

Moreover, work and nonwork balance has become a concern among public policy-makers and international institutions (particularly in the European Union but also at the United Nation). These policy-makers and institutions provide guidelines and models for stakeholders that address this issue in the workplace and in society in general. They also give particular attention to gender equality and life balance concerns of parents and caregivers for older people. Similarly, the issue of pregnancy discrimination in the workplace is one of the most evident examples of "imbalance" that has been regulated in several countries such as the United States, United Kingdom, EU, and Australia. Special Focus Box 7.2 shows an example of a policy developed by a local public administration in Italy with the goal of encouraging fathers' involvement in the care of children with working mothers. This example shows how, through public policies and public monies, institutions can try to alleviate the family-work conflict for couples with young children and, at the same time, balance family burdens across caregivers.

Special Focus Box 7.2: Public Policy to Encourage Fathers in Childcare Activities

The Administration provides financial support to foster greater use of parental leave by the father as an alternative to the working mother for the care of children under the age of 12.

For the period in which parental leave is requested, the mother must be self-employed or employed. Mothers must carry out their work starting from the beginning of the use of parental leave of the father and for the entire duration of the financial support.

The Administration recognizes fathers who use parental leave as an alternative to the working mother, and provides financial support of €350 for every 15 consecutive days of parental leave taken, for a maximum of four months (120 days) for each child.

Work-Nonwork Balance Across the Lifespan

Work-nonwork balance issues change across the lifespan in concert with changes in working experiences, changes in the family situation, and changes in interests and abilities both at and away from work. Across the life course, people experience change in their work/career demands, the demands of parenthood, and often the demands associated with parental or grandchild caregiving. Further, as people age their attention tends to shift from career issues to the development of a satisfying life outside of work and after they retire. Obviously, people develop skills and strategies that allow them to handle these changes in different domains, but the evolving – and often abrupt – nature of changes in work and home life can be disconcerting and create feelings of stress, requiring accommodations both at work and away from work to maintain balance. Consequently, the conditions for nurturing balance between life domains are evolving over the lifespan. This issue does not concern the chronological age of a person in itself. Rather, it involves the evolution of opportunities, challenges, and problems that people encounter at different life stages; and with this, the need to recreate balance among the domains of work, family, leisure, social, community, and political activities, and spiritual life.

Thinking about how the *work career* intersects the lifespan, many scholars have tried to define different stages in which careers can evolve over the course of life. One of the most established and influential models is that of Super (1957; 1980)[4]:

Exploration (typical age: 15–24): building the professional self-concept and identify occupations that fit with it; in this phase people develop the career choices, explore the first work opportunities and develop the work-entry competences;

Establishment (typical age 25–45): acquisition of a stable job position, followed by professional development and progressive adjustment of the professional self;

Maintenance (typical age 45–65): career stabilization, constant updating of skills and competencies according to the technological and organizational changes taking place;

Disengagement (typical age 55–65+): preparation to the exit phase, decreasing involvement in organizational life.

This classic definition of career stage can be a useful simplification to understand the different approaches to career at different stages in the lifespan.

However, these stages are quite variable and sensitive to changes in social and organizational contexts. Think at the following examples: the increases in the age at which many people begin their careers due obtaining college and graduate degrees; the delays in retirement due to increases in the legal retirement age; the multiple careers that people can have during their life in the dynamic occupational context in our historical period. For these reasons, today is really difficult to define precise career stages with very clear "typical ages" that could be valid for a large number of workers. The more recent career scientists[5] are inclined to consider the career as:

- *Boundaryless:* high level of mobility and many transitions between organizations;
- *Protean:* numerous changes, due to the evolution of people's interests and talents over the course of their lives;
- *Nonlinear:* development over time not necessarily of vertical ascent but characterized by horizontal transitions, blocks and changes of direction.

That means a larger individual mobility between organizations, a stronger self-management of career choices, a less regular and less predictable career development in the lifespan. All these emerging characteristics of the careers are also reflected in the management of work-nonwork balance organizational policies. Those who plan and manage these organizational interventions will have to devote individualized attention to how individuals' needs, expectations and career aspirations change over the course of their lives, as will be recalled at the end of the chapter.

The complexity improves if we think about the life course associated with *family dynamics*. It is quickly apparent that there is even more variability in paths and experiences, depending on gender, education, job aspirations, culture, religious beliefs, and other factors. However, analyzing the situation of a couple with children, one can think of a series of phases that differentially impact the working domain:

Launching: a phase of construction of the family nucleus and planning of children;

Parenthood: a parenthood phase that coincides with the children's pre-school and school age;

Empty nest: a period in which children leave their family of origin, although in many cases they maintain a certain economic dependence on their parents.

The steps described above are rather broad and generic, and it is possible to consider different transitional phases.[6] For example, the *launching* phase could be more or less long and could even lead to the decision not to have children. The broad phase of childcare (*parenthood*) has very different temporal and organizational needs during the first years of the child's life (early parenthood) or the adolescent and post-adolescence period. And *becoming parents* usually is a very critical transition stage with the need to regulate several changes in family and work life: restructuring life time for caring for young babies; negotiating the reciprocal responsibility within the couple; managing the financial pressure due to the increased demand for household goods and services. All these changes in the family domain – which on the one hand subtract psychological resources, but on the other require more material resources – can have repercussions on the working sphere (intensity of the performance; level of attention; level of engagement) and on organizational commitment (availability for work; organizational identification). The potential high risk of work-family conflict persists also during the *preschool age*.

With the growth of *children in school age and adolescence*, the load of potential work-family conflict tends to decrease as some basic needs for care and support are mitigated. The children gradually become more autonomous, even if new needs emerge, related to school choices, friendship groups, socio-cognitive, and emotional development during the adolescence of the children. For example, it may be more difficult to implement a transfer for work if adolescent children have friendships and social activities that are well-rooted in a geographic area.

The stage called *"empty nest"* in fact can also include those situations in which adult children continue to live in their family of origin. This is a widespread phenomenon in some southern European countries and growing even in the Anglo-Saxon countries and in United States (about 24 million 18- to 34-year-olds, lived in their parents' home in 2015).[7]

From this brief description, it is clear that there are phases of life in which important tasks and potentially conflicting demands co-occur between working life (in the phase of full development and with strong motivational investment) and family life (also in a time of growth and with strong affective involvement). It is in these phases of the life cycle that the drain of resources and energies from both contexts (work and family) is greater. See Special Focus Box 7.3.

However, an emerging issue concerns the mature phase of working couples. Very often the older worker shifts their extra-work attention to their parents who, having grown old and who are gradually losing their

Special Focus Box 7.3: Some Scientific Evidence

In the scientific psychological literature is possible to find some confirmation, based on evidence, that older workers manage work and nonwork domains in a different way compared to younger workers. Allen and Finkelstein found that older workers report lower level of work/nonwork interference. In two other different studies (Spieler et al.), older workers reported better work-life balance. In both studies, older workers, compared to young workers, achieve higher work-life balance and less interference by actively managing work-nonwork boundaries to keep life domains more separated.

Allen, T., & Finkelstein, L. M. (2014). Work-family conflict among members of full-time dual earner couples: An examination of family life stage, gender, and age. *Journal of Occupational Health Psychology, 19*, 376–384.

Spieler, I., Scheibe, S., & Stamov Roßnagel, C. (2018). Keeping work and private life apart: Age-related differences in managing the work-nonwork interface. *Journal of Organizational Behavior, 39*, 1233–1251.

autonomy and need assistance and care. This eldercare activity is often provided by people still working and sometimes it is added to the economic and logistical support they provide for their children. This creates a *"sandwich"* situation where a mature worker might provide care to their parents and provide services and money to their children who are at the beginning of their professional career or still engaged in higher education.

In summary, two important messages we must keep from this paragraph to use them in a logic of organizational interventions:

- There is a large variability *between* people in work-nonwork balance during the lifespan (i.e., conflicts can happen in different life stages for different people);
- There is a high level of *change over time* in the life experience of people (i.e., in different life stage people can experience different needs and conflicts).

Work-Life Balance and Organizational Interventions

An organization's human resource policies can also play an important role in assisting employees to develop better work-nonwork balance. Work organizations can intervene to reduce the potential for work-family conflict and to improve interchange between these two areas of life. These interventions, generally called *"family friendly"*, can have positive effects on the quality of life of workers, but also on increasing organizational productivity and reducing absenteeism.

The typology of organizational interventions is quite varied; often the interventions are impromptu and lacking a specific evidence-based evaluation regarding the results and benefits produced (a PIERA model is generally not followed).

Trying to formulate an approximate classification of human resource policies aimed at the reduction of work-nonwork conflict, based on programs that have a scientific evaluation basis,[8] we can distinguish three broad families of organizational interventions.

a. *Care arrangements*: the organization provides services and benefits to workers that can improve the balance between work and family and work and leisure; interventions such as paid parental leave, onsite childcare, health and fitness facilities fall into this category;

b. *Time management*: organizational interventions aimed at facilitating nonwork life through the management of working hours. This is the type of intervention that is probably the most widely used and with a variety of approaches: telecommuting; flexible working hours; different models of shiftwork; rotation within the teamwork; compressed work weeks (e.g., four-day work week);

c. *Training for supervisors and employees*: deeper organizational interventions may involve changes in organizational culture and leadership development (see Special Focus Box 7.4). These interventions aim to give greater awareness, through managerial and supervisor training on organizational policies, as well the importance of work-life balance to employee well-being and how to model and support work-life balance among employees.

Some studies[9] have also identified a causal relationship between workplace flexibility policies in late career employment and retirement decisions and exit strategies. Time and place management initiatives (flexibility on when and where to work) seem to have a positive impact on workers' expectations and their intention to remain in the organization throughout the late career. These scientific results seem to confirm the possible positive outcomes of initiatives such as those described in the case in Special Focus Box 7.6.

The Special Focus Box 7.5 contains some reflections on how the COVID-19 pandemic has affected the balance between work and family.

Special Focus Box 7.4: Leadership and Work-Nonwork Balance

There is evidence that a "respectful leader", interested in the employees demands and needs, may help minimize conflicts between work and nonwork life by giving the employees more control in managing working time. Also, the feeling of being treated respectfully may result in less negative spillovers from work to private life.

This respectful attitude of the leader can have then positive and indirect effects on motivation and intention to continue to work for older workers. Low work-nonwork conflict is likely to reduce older workers' desired retirement age. High work-nonwork conflict improves the role pressure and consequently the intention to quit and to anticipate the retirement age.

Wöhrmann, A. M., Fasbender, U., & Deller, J. (2017). Does more respect from leaders postpone the desire to retire? Understanding the mechanisms of retirement decision making. *Frontiers in Psychology*, 8.

Special Focus Box 7.5: Work-Nonwork Balance and COVID-19

The COVID-19 pandemic has had a significant impact on the balance between working life and nonworking life. Unfortunately, scientific studies on the subject are currently still scarce, but some critical areas can be guessed from what we already know in this area. In these critical areas, managerial interventions will have to focus in the coming months or maybe years.

1. E-work. The pandemic and its lockdown have prompted many workers to operate remotely, from home and with interactions mediated by new technologies. In many cases, remote work was forced by circumstances and the organizational preparation for managing e-work was rushed and done urgently. Organizational interventions are necessary to:
   a. better define how to work remotely (how to operate by objectives; how to self-control the time of work);
   b. train staff (e.g., training on the use of new technologies to work in remote teams, particularly for older workers);
   c. deal with new forms stress (feeling of social isolation, cognitive overload);
   d. evaluate performance and preserve quality and innovation.

2. Interference with family loads. The pandemic and the lockdown, in addition to forcing people to work remotely, have also seriously disturbed the organization of social life within families. The closure of schools and activities for young people has meant that the e-work of adults has overlapped with more intense family care of children. Work responsibilities and family care have become more simultaneous. The work of caring for the children was also amplified by social isolation; the role of family support of grandparents and other family members was lacking. It is evident that this situation of "interference" between e-work and family load management is more marked in couples with young children. Organizational solutions can mitigate these interferences, such as giving the possibility of doing work remotely at atypical times (early in the morning and in the evening), although obviously these situations can interfere with the provision of services and the need to synchronize with other colleagues.

3. Work-health balance. A third element concerns the balance between working life and individual health. Here things have changed dramatically, especially for older workers. COVID-19 mortality is known to be higher among those over 60 and that the most serious effects of the virus are for older people. Older workers are more vulnerable to the pandemic. This means that personnel management policies will necessarily have to deal with protecting these fragile subjects to a greater extent.

Rudolph, C. et al. (in press). Pandemics: implications for research and practice in industrial and organizational psychology. *Industrial and Organizational Psychology. Perspectives on Science and Practice.* See also this recent paper: https://www.shrm.org/hr-today/news/all-things-work/Pages/covid-19-deals-a-dual-threat-to-older-workers.aspx.

Special Focus Box 7.6: Case Study. Project Per.La – Personalization of Working Hours in a Public Health Service Organization

The company: The "APSS" is an Italian public healthcare organizations with more than 7,700 employees, serving around 500 thousand members of the public. This includes the direct management of 7 hospitals, 13 health districts, 3 structural departments, and an operating budget of around one billion euros. About 70% of APSS's workers are female. Like all public healthcare organizations, APSS provides services 24 hours a day, 365 days a year. Thus, it is easy to see how the organization of APSS's work could affect employees' private lives.

The needs analysis: The project Per.La (personalization of working hours) is the result of a preliminary study on working time problems at APSS. In the past, employees were forced to adopt some contractual changes to balance their professional and personal lives, which were part-time solutions or furloughs. However, these solutions produced difficulties in organizing work. Part time was considered an unfair measure for reconciling work and nonwork: it limits access to career development, and it has negative effects on salary and retirement benefits.

Furloughs were applied for reasons related to maternity and breastfeeding. Moreover, during the summer period of closing of the educational institutions, other staff made use of the furloughs for family reasons. Thus, a considerable portion of staff did not contribute continuously to the activity of the APSS, producing organizational dysfunction and perceptions of unfairness related to the distribution of workload. However, it was believed that the introduction of flexible working hours would facilitate work-nonwork balance. This was the rationale of the Per.La project.

The aims of the project: The project Per.La aimed to promote forms of flexibility in the working hours of employees so as to guarantee a more balanced relationship between working life and personal life. The project, intended for non-shift workers, administrative, technical and health personnel, was to improve the quality of the working life of the staff, implementing a particularly flexible system that allowed people to organize working time in response to their outside needs. The solutions were tailored to address both the individual needs and the organizational constraints, after an individual negotiation process. The Per.La project was approved and partially funded by the Prime Minister's Family Policy Department.

The Expected Results

Customization of working hours and working methods that would meet the needs of workers and increase their productivity at work;

Identification of a system of consistent and "do-able" good practices that would extend this system to all employees;

Increase in employee satisfaction;

Reduction of absenteeism and requests to decrease working hours (furloughs);

Improvement in the career opportunities of those employees who, because they use the flexibility program, do not provide a constant presence in the company;

Increase in the quality of the service provided to the public.

People Involved

The staff (health workers and non-medical non-shift workers) with minor children, or family members or elderly people who are disabled or not self-sufficient. The project involved more than 230 employees.

The managers responsible for the structures who were directly involved in the negotiation of the agreements. To find the most suitable forms of customization for people and services involved, steps were also taken to reorganize the offices, services, and work processes.

The unions were kept constantly updated on the project and results.

The Interventions Adopted

The method used is the decentralized agreement, that is, negotiated and signed between the individual employee and manager. Those who participated in the project had to share their personalized timetables with colleagues and managers, with the goal of addressing the needs of the individual, those of the group, and those of the APSS.

The types of timetables agreed were very different for different employees, depending on their needs and the needs of their work unit:

a) Minimal adjustments. This would include changing the times that the employee was required to come to work or could leave work, or expanding the range of arrival and departure times available to the employee.

b) Management of working hours independently, ensuring compliance with a weekly or monthly number of hours. This might also involve establishing of one or more time slots of mandatory presence at work. The remainder of the time spent at work by the employee would be up to the individual organization.

c) Different variable working hours plans, to be utilized according to the contingent needs (family and work) of employees. This would require prior communication to the manager and to other colleagues of the specific work hours and for which work period (week or month).

d) In all cases, the provision of services, opening hours to the public, and availability of employees were always maintained.

Some Examples

Gigliola is a 40-year-old administrative assistant and mother of two children aged 7 and 5. She commutes about 30 km to work every day. She doesn't have a family network that can help her manage the family. She personalized her working hours as follows: flexible arrival time from 8.00 to 9.00, which allows her to accompany her children to school; working hours structured as "long" days (3) and "short" days (2); one day a week (usually Friday) she telecommutes from home.

Paola is a 55-year-old administrative assistant. She travels about 40 km every day to go to work. Her 90-year-old mother lives with her and needs assistance. She customized her working hours to include flexibility with regard to arrival time and working from home, which is available to her up to three days a week. She can also use both full days, or she can use split days to complete the day.

The Unit of Physical Medicine and Rehabilitation has introduced the customization of working hours to address the organization's needs, specifically, in order to respond to the needs of the public who requested services outside normal service hours (i.e., before 8.00 and after 16.00, and in particular to meet their work commitments). An appointment (45 minutes) was added to the normal working hours of the physiotherapist in the "extreme" bands, that is, before 7.00 am or 4.00 pm. This employee recovers these hours by taking off whole days periods with less demand for services.

Monitoring and Evaluation

The intermediate and final monitoring of the experiment made it possible to record some positive results with regard to the satisfaction of the employees, the impact on the services, and on the organization as a whole. The project triggered:

1. a change in organizational culture, transforming the needs of work-nonwork balance into something that has become an integral part of the culture of the organization;
2. a decrease in absences and overtime (−3.4% of absences for maternity and childcare and 409 hours of overtime in a year of project);
3. an upswing of working hours, with the return to full-time of 16 people, including 14 women (about 30% of the part-time project participants);
4. an increase in individual autonomy, taking responsibility and the ability to find/develop solutions for managing the employee's own working/family time.

Given the positive results, the Per.La project was adopted as a permanent organizational practice. To date, it has involved around 700 people who negotiated customized hourly solutions. These are mainly women (75%) and employees aged between 45 and 55 (50%), but also with a significant number of employees over 55 (17%).

The PIERA Approach to a Work-Nonwork Balance Intervention

How can you plan for an organizational invention to improve work-nonwork balance? The examples of organizational interventions presented above are taken from experiences often reported in scientific journals or reports of personnel management policies. In many cases, these are experimental studies where at least short-term. However, these interventions must be considered with a critical eye and in the light of what was previously described (Chapter 2) regarding the *PIERA* model.

Planning

First, many of the solutions listed above are not planned according to the needs of people of different ages, career stages, and family characteristics. For example, the advantages of a compressed working week, based on 4 days of intensive work, can be appreciated by those who want to dedicate longer weekends to their leisure, but can hinder the daily activities of those who assist a sick parent or for people with young children at school. Applying the *P* (Planning) of PIERA, one should first investigate the specific needs of people to whom the intervention will be applied, and then customize the intervention so that it fits the needs of all workers. The case study at the end of this chapter is an example of this "idiosyncratic deals" approach.

Implementation

Second, one should consider concerns with implementation (the *I* of PIERA) of the intervention within the complex organizational system. Simply applying a "family friendly" policy, without taking into consideration the potential effects on the entire organizational system, can create more damage than benefits. Persons excluded from the intervention (e.g., those who do not have children of preschool age, in the case of a company kindergarten project) may perceive unfairness: the organization invests resources in workers with young children and ignores the needs of those who have other needs (e.g., medical care for chronic diseases). This perception of organizational injustice can have potential negative effects on performance and motivation and create hostility between groups of workers. Moreover, from the other side, sometimes those who benefit from "family friendly" policies (e.g., telecommuting or flexible working hours) can have fewer career opportunities, be allocated to lower level job roles or responsibilities. Further, the implementation phase of an intervention must consider all these possible counterproductive effects and must find solutions to prevent perceptions of injustice, feelings of discrimination, and feelings of deprivation. Rather, the goal should be to find a solution that is perceived as fair and beneficial to all workers, as is shown in the case study at the end of this chapter.

Evaluation, Reflection, Adjustment

Only with an accurate evaluation (the *E* of PIERA) and a deep analysis of the information collected (Reflection; the *R* of PIERA) can managers be prepared for an adjustment (the *A* of PIERA) of the intervention and an improvement of the individual and organizational outcomes.

Action Items: Things to Do Right Now, Next Week, and Long Term

Things to Do Now

Check if the things you've read are clear enough and are applicable to your organization. Do you think that the balance between working life and extra-working life is a relevant issue for your work organization? Do you have to make decisions that can affect people's life balance (e.g., establishing shifts and asking for time availability)? What criteria have you worked with to make these decisions so far?

Things to Do Next Week

Check if the staff working with you have people or groups of people particularly exposed to the conflict between working life and extra-working life. Analyzes gender, age, health conditions, family situation as possible elements to be taken into consideration.

Things to Do Long Term

If the working life-nonworking life interface is an important element for the proper functioning of your business and if you have identified groups of people most exposed to potential conflict (women, older workers, people with serious family difficulties), then elaborate on possible organizational solutions (e.g., more flexibility in time and space management). Discuss these possible solutions with stakeholders and within teams. Remember that it is important to preserve a high perception of organizational equity.

Notes

1. For a meta-analysis see: Amstad, F. T., Meier, L. L., Fasel, U., Elfering, A., & Semmer, N. K. (2011). A meta-analysis of work–family conflict and various outcomes with a special emphasis on cross-domain versus matching-domain relations. *Journal of Occupational Health Psychology, 16*(2), 151–169.
2. Nohe, C., Meier, L. L., Sonntag, K., Michel, A. (2015). The chicken or the egg? A meta-analysis of panel studies of the relationship between work-family conflict and strain. *Journal of Applied Psychology, 100*, 522–536.
3. Nussbaum M. C. (2009). Liberty of conscience: The attack on equal respect. *Journal of Human Development and Capabilities, 8*, 337–357.
4. Super, D. E. (1957). *The psychology of careers*. New York: Harper and Row; Super, D. E. (1980). A life-span, life-space approach to career development. *Journal of Vocational Behavior, 13*, 282–298.
5. Arthur, M. B., & Rousseau, D. M. (Eds.). (1996). *The boundaryless career: A new employment principle for a new organizational era*. New York: Oxford University Press; Hall, D. T. (2004). The protean career. A quarter-century journey. *Journal of Vocational Behavior, 65*, 1–13; Lichtenstein, B., & Mendenhall, M. (2002). Non-linearity and response-ability: Emergent order in 21st century careers. *Human Relations, 55*, 5–32.
6. See for a more detailed analysis: Clark, M. A., Sanders, K. N., Haynes, N. J., & Vande Griek, O. H. (2019). Lifespan perspectives on work and nonwork roles. In B. B. Baltes, C. W. Rudolph, & H. Zacher (Eds.), *Work across lifespan* (pp. 395–416). London: Academic Press.
7. https://www.census.gov/content/dam/Census/library/publications/2017/demo/p20-579.pdf
8. Brough, P., & O'Driscoll, M. P. (2010). Organizational interventions for balancing work and home demands: An overview. *Work & Stress, 24*(3), 280–297; Hammer, L. B., Kossek, E. E., Anger, W. K., Bodner, T., & Zimmerman, K. L. (2011). Clarifying work-family intervention processes: The roles of work-family conflict and family-supportive supervisor behaviors. *Journal of Applied Psychology, 96*, 134–150.
9. Cahill, K. E., James, J. B., Pitt-Catsouphes, M. (2015). The impact of a randomly assigned time and place management initiative on work and retirement expectations. *Work Aging and Retirement, 1*(4), 350–368.

Managing and Supporting Employee Talent for Success and Satisfaction Across the Lifespan

8

Talent retention is most certainly a buzz-phrase in most organizations and for good reason. It is imperative for organizations to hold on to and develop their top employees. But we know that keeping the best folks can be an uphill battle in today's competitive market. Although there are plenty of resources out there that discuss talent management and especially talent retention, developing and retaining the best employees *over the course of their lifespan* are not a commonly addressed. Those resources that do tread into this area often use that generation simplification we warned you about in Chapter 1 (e.g., "Here's how to attract and keep the top Millennial employees!"). Despite what we hear in the media, Millennials don't each have identical needs – they are individuals – plus members of any generation will change over time.

In this chapter we will introduce some basic concepts of talent development and retention, while focusing most on the specific issues that our lifespan perspective brings to light. We address the topics of how to assess talent and needs, provide feedback, and create career development paths with an eye on aging. We also stress potential differences in how employees evolve over the lifespan: not all people age at work in the same way, and a focus on *chronological age* does not paint a complete picture about the resources and needs of workers. We provide some insights and advice about how you can use the PIERA strategy to put a lens of lifespan development on your own talent management approaches.

We have chosen to focus this talent chapter mostly on the *retention* component of talent management. We believe we would be remiss, however, if we entirely ignored the role age could play in the initial aspects of the talent management cycle, including recruitment and hiring. We provide a few notes on these potential issues in Special Focus Box 8.1.

Special Focus Box 8.1: Thoughts on Age, Recruitment, and Hiring

Whether or not you work in a country with laws that prevent discrimination based on age, it is wise to avoid recruitment and selection practices that would unfairly limit the pool of talent because of intentional or inadvertent bias. Whereas most HR professionals and hiring managers actively try to avoid biases against other protected groups, age may not always get the same consideration. Consider the following:

- Studies have consistently shown very little predictable difference in job performance in relation to age – people don't necessarily get better or get worse with age.
- You may inadvertently reduce your potential qualified applicant pool by advertising jobs only on websites that are used disproportionately by younger people.
- Certain language in job ads (e.g., "fast-paced", "vigorous") may signal to some older workers that they would not be considered for a job that they may have been great for, leading you to lose some potential talent.
- Some language that applicants use in resumes may trigger age stereotypes for some recruiters, leading them to reject good resumes in a screening process.
- Look at the selection ratio (number hired/number in pool) of older applicants as compared to younger applicants. If it is considerably lower, it could be because:
  - Decision-makers are using an implicit or explicit age bias in their choices.
  - Assessments being used to aid selection, such as cognitive ability, physical ability, or personality tests may show *disparate impact* – one age group is either scoring lower than the other consistently, or those assessments are less predictive of job performance in one group or the other.

- The administration of selection assessments is not equally user-friendly for one group compared to the other (e.g., some app-based assessments).
- You may be actively seeking to hire applicants across the lifespan, but actually attracting only a particular group. Applicants try to match their own needs, strengths, and self-image to what they are learning about the job and the organization. It may be that your recruitment strategies are signaling a clear fit for applicants at some life stages more than others.

Derous, E., & Decoster, J. (2017). Implicit age cues in resumes: Subtle effects on hiring discrimination. *Frontiers in Psychology, 8*, 1–15.

Fisher, G. G., Truxillo, D. M., Finkelstein, L. M., & Wallace, L. E. (2016). Age discrimination: Potential for adverse impact and differential prediction related to age. *Human Resource Management Review, 27*, 316–327.

Rudolph, C. W., Toomey, E. C., & Baltes, B. B. (2017). Considering age diversity in recruitment and selection: An expanded work lifespan view of age management. In E. Parry & J. McCarthy (Eds.), *The Palgrave handbook of age diversity and work* (pp. 607–638). London: Palgrave.

Assessment of Talent

If the focus of talent retention is to hold on to the best employees for the long haul across their career trajectories and lifespans, it is essential to consider how you identify who is "best". An accurate process for assessing talent is paramount. The first step is to determine what "talent" means to your organization. There are different philosophies when it comes to talent, and gauging where your organization stands on the whole idea of talent is essential. There is one camp that believes that talent signifies those who are the top performers in the company. This might be those that are considered "best of the best" in each functional area, or may focus most specifically on those in what are sometimes called *pivotal positions* – those positions where even slight increases in performance can have major impact on the organization. This is an *exclusionary approach* in the sense that you are looking to find current top performers who have the highest potential to make a big splash in the future. In a way, it is sorting the haves from have-nots to determine who should get the lion's share of resources and developmental attention.

At the other end of the spectrum is a more *inclusionary approach*, where all employees are considered talent. If they were carefully selected into the organization, they can contribute and reach their own highest potential. With this view, you are not comparing people to each other, but rather to their best selves.[1] This approach resonates with the philosophies and assumptions of positive psychology, where everyone has a unique combination of strengths and passions that can be nurtured for the greater good.

Of course, there is a middle ground, where the top is still identified but resources go to everyone to maximize performance and engagement across the board. A strictly exclusionary approach may send a negative message to the majority of employees that they are not worth developing and investing in – this could generate risk to losing members of your essential workforce. It also may create a negative organizational culture.

Understanding your organization's foundational outlook on talent will help determine who should be assessed, how often, and for what.[2] But, whether it's to determine who gets special opportunities or to figure out how to get the most out of all your employees, there are a host of decisions where having a lifespan lens can help.

Talent Assessment Across the Age Span

Assessment practices are central to determining abilities and skill sets. The focus likely depends on the employee's functional area but may include cognitive abilities, leadership skills, interpersonal or customer skills, learning agility, computer or software savvy, to name a few.[3] These may be assessed with validated objective tests, or they may be determined through a regular performance appraisal process using the subjective ratings of supervisors or sometimes even peers and subordinates in a 360-degree appraisal, or perhaps a combination. For example, assessment centers for managers sometimes include written tests, but then also put employees in many different work-relevant situations and have trained raters judge their performance.[4]

What does an employee's age or career stage have to do with this? First, if the assessment is being conducted to determine whether the employee should be classified as high potential, be aware that the idea of *potential* implies something in the future, and therefore stereotypically tends to be associated with younger people. It could be that mid-life or older workers who may have potential for growing further into a position – or even have the needed skills already – get overlooked even for the opportunity to be considered because they don't fit the image of what "potential" looks like.[5]

Continuing with the idea of age stereotypes, are any of the other competencies being assessed typically associated with a particular age group? For example, is it assumed a younger person won't have the communication skills needed to interact with established clients? Do we expect that our older employee doesn't know how to use the latest social media platform? As we touched on in Chapter 6, it is natural for us to have these stereotypes, and they are so ubiquitous in our everyday culture that we don't even notice them springing into action. What's more, we also have a human tendency to look for evidence to confirm our beliefs and to ignore contradictory information. Although we can't erase all our biases, an awareness of them can help.

Any of the more objective assessments we may choose, such as tests, should always be vetted to insure they are not only good predictors of performance, but also have been examined for illegal bias, including age bias. Test publishers will typically report in their user's manuals the studies that they have done to look for differential impact of their tests, but age information tends to be less common that that for other groups, such as gender and race. Cognitive tests that are timed and focus more on what's called the fluid aspect of intelligence (e.g., reasoning and problem solving in novel situations) may exhibit adverse impact with older employees as compared with those that assess the crystalized aspects of intelligence (e.g., acquired knowledge).[6]

With the intention of retaining talent, we want to go beyond assessment of competencies – the *can do* elements – and also look at what people *want to do*. What are their intentions and dreams for their future career? And, in reading that last sentence, were you picturing a young employee at the start of a career when you think of things like "dreams" and "futures"? As careers unfold, some interests and motives may change (see Chapter 3). Employees may want to shift to new areas or expand their scope or make a difference in a new way. But don't assume this is automatically happening at some magical age for your employees. Rather, keep a pulse of how people may want to grow or shift in the way they make contributions to the organization. If the goal is to hold on to talent throughout their career, assessing desires as well as skills, and keeping this information up to date and top of mind when opportunities arise will go a long way. Some retention professionals recommend regular "stay interviews" to collect data on what will help employees stay loyal to the organization.[7]

Assessment data, as mentioned, can be used for various purposes including high potential designation, succession planning, decision-making for assigning developmental opportunities, and promotions. These data need to be distributed to the appropriate parties to maximize their use; a key recipient of that information is the employee themselves. In the following section, we discuss giving feedback to employees and the lifespan issues pertinent to this process.

Feedback

"I think you need to give some feedback to John about his recent perform-ance", is a sentence that might evoke a twinge of dread in the heart of a manager, as would "John, can you stop by later? I've got some feedback for you". Truth is, the ideas of both giving and receiving feedback can trigger unpleasantness. Is feedback a necessary evil, is it really useless, or can it actually be part and parcel of an engaging work environment? All of those can be true, and we want to focus on how to achieve the latter. Further – as it's really why we're here – we want to focus on the role age might play in the acceptance and utility of feedback and what that should mean for planning feedback policies and practices as part of a larger talent retention strategy.

Before we go any further, what exactly do we mean by feedback? What first comes to mind may be something like the scenario imagined above – a supervisor sitting a subordinate down in their office to tell them that their performance is not up to par. In their popular book *Thanks for the Feedback*, Stone and Heen describe feedback very simply as "any information you get about yourself".[8] This information may be about performance, but it could also be about attitudes, commitment to the team, communica-tion style, reputation, or professionalism, to name a few. It could be given formally as part of an annual performance review process, but it could also be given informally in the course of a chat by the coffee machine. It could be given with a direct statement, or perhaps an implied hint. It might come not from verbal communication at all, but from seeing an eye-roll or hearing a loosely-veiled excuse to hastily leave a conversation. It could come from above, below, or anywhere in between.

Feedback happens all of the time, in forms that can ignite positive changes or trigger a downward spiral. The good news is that science has uncovered ways to increase the likelihood that feedback will have the intended effects and be a part of the fabric of a strong organization. Taking

Special Focus Box 8.2: The Benefits of Feedback Done Well

- *Task motivation:* people can react to negative feedback by striving to reduce the gap between what they do (actual performance) and what is expected from them (desired performance).
- *Task learning:* people can learn effective skills and behaviors and can prevent or discourage ineffective behaviors.
- *Focused attention:* people can concentrate greater focus on their most important work objectives and better monitor the execution of their task.
- *Perspective taking:* people can gain understanding of what others in the organization (coworkers, supervisors, clients) are feeling, thinking, and expecting. This can help them look beyond their own frames of reference and biases.
- *Self-confidence:* people gain evidence that they and their work are valued by others and that they are headed in the right direction.

Kluger, A. N., & DeNisi, A. (1996). The effects of feedback interventions on performance: A historical review, a meta-analysis, and a preliminary feedback intervention theory. *Psychological Bulletin, 119,* 254–284.

Sherf, E. N., & Morrison, E. W. (2020). I do not need feedback! Or do I? Self-efficacy, perspective taking, and feedback seeking. *Journal of Applied Psychology, 105,* 146–165.

into account, the context and the particular characteristics of the individuals in that context (including, but not over relying on age, of course) are elemental parts of the strategy.

In case you need any more convincing, the tool of feedback – when wielded deftly – has a number of functions. Check out Special Focus Box 8.2 for some specifics.

If these potential benefits of feedback come to fruition, employees are focusing more of their time and attention on their most important tasks and roles, conscious of and working toward continual improvement, and seeing where their work fits into the big picture and how they are viewed by their team. But if the feedback is seen as threatening to their position, or sometimes even to their identity[9] (for instance, if someone fancies themselves a true wordsmith, and then receives a returned draft marked to the hilt in red), then the feedback may be ignored. Let's look at some general factors that might enhance the acceptance of feedback, and then address when and how an employee's age should factor into a feedback approach.

First, when feedback is *only* provided in the context of formal performance appraisals, its rarity may overemphasize the feeling that it is a high-stakes event to be feared and endured, not embraced as potentially useful. In some organizations and among some cynical folks, there is a belief (which in some cases may be true) that the process is riddled with organizational politics (e.g., a supervisor providing inflated information to make themselves look good).[10]

On the other hand, there are conditions under which feedback can be quite beneficial in organizations:

- If a workplace has an open feedback culture where it is provided regularly, with a clear standard of performance expectations and in an open and constructive manner, it may be expected and taken in stride.[11] Moreover, when those performance appraisal days do come around, the jitters may be taken down a few notches.[12]
- There is evidence to suggest that providing feedback in a considerate way and with welcomed and active participation of the recipient does make a positive difference in the way it is received, but those behaviors themselves might not be enough.
- The relationship within which the feedback is exchanged should be one that is strong, trusting, and supportive to increase the likelihood that feedback will be taken to heart.[13] If leaders are making efforts to build strong relationships with their team members and showing them that they tuned in to each of their unique strengths and opportunities for growth, feedback is more likely to be received with open ears.

There are some additional issues that to consider when providing feedback:

- Even when supervisory relationship and organization conditions are favorable, employees will differ on their likelihood to seek out feedback, their emotional reaction to it, and their ability to translate it into positive action. Paying close attention to each of your employees' proclivities in relation to feedback can help you craft the right message for the individual.
- Leaders may find they are giving feedback to some people more than others. One reason may be that some employees seek it out more often than others. A culture that emphasizes the value of multiple and diverse perspectives can encourage people to seek out feedback more often.[14]

- Although we want employees to feel safe to seek out feedback and see its value, leaders also need to be forthright in providing it. Research reveals, for example, some unconscious biases in the way feedback is communicated to men as compared with women, leading women to end up with less direct feedback for advancement.[15]

What Role Does Age Play in Feedback Reactions?

Because we are interested in understanding how people of different ages and in different career stages might react differently to performance feedback, we need to classify feedback *orientations* and *characteristics*. *Feedback orientation* describes how, in general terms, an individual receives feedback and assesses it. Research has uncovered two specific orientations that have shown some differences when it comes to the age of employees:

- *Social awareness*: their tendency to use feedback to understand the point of view of others about their performance in order to interpret the quality of their relationships at work;
- *Utility*: their tendency to use feedback instrumentally in order to improve their performance and achieve their performance goals.

Although scientists have only begun to look at age differences in feedback orientation, one key study demonstrated that older workers tend to have a higher social awareness orientation and lower utility orientation as compared to younger workers.[16] The reasoning is that younger workers tend to be earlier in their career and are trying to get very specific feedback to help them be successful in their performance in order to advance professionally. In contrast, older workers tend to have a clearer understanding of their performance and abilities and might value the contributions they are making to the social fabric of their workplace.

Of course, "tend to" is a very deliberate phrasing in this explanation. First, these trends are just that – trends – and based on an assumption that older workers are experienced in their current job. In certain cases they could be newer workers who are just learning too. Or it could be that any one particular worker is and always will be very performance-driven throughout their career – and even if they come to value the relational aspects of work more and more over the course of her life, their high-performance orientation could exceed that of a younger person who just happens to value balance and other aspects of life over moving up the ladder.

Having said that, these data suggest that in giving employees feedback, considering the age and career stage of the recipient could be one useful factor when crafting a feedback message. More senior workers may be paying attention to and valuing information concerning the relational aspects of the feedback, while younger and less seasoned workers may seek more information that is actionable for enhancing their performance and professional growth toward a more central role in the organization.

Recall the second aspect of feedback we mentioned above was *feedback characteristics;* this same research indicates that this may also be valued differently as workers evolve over their life course. Some key feedback characteristics include:

- *Favorability*: whether the feedback is perceived as being positive ("my supervisor let me know that I was doing a good job") or negative ("my supervisor pointed out my mistakes").
- *Delivery*: the manner in which the feedback is given and how the source of feedback is perceived in terms of empathy and tact ("my supervisor was considerate of my feelings when giving me performance feedback").
- *Quality*: whether the feedback is perceived as consistent, detailed, and constructive ("the feedback I received from my supervisor gave me specific ideas for doing more job more efficiently").

The previously mentioned study found that:

- Older workers tended to react more positively to feedback favorability characteristics, valuing the positivity of the feedback as a source of reinforcement of their self-image.
- Older workers also tended to react more positively to feedback delivery characteristics, valuing the interpersonal aspects of the feedback more than do younger workers.
- In contrast, younger workers tended to react more positively than older workers to the quality of feedback, preferring to receive relevant, consistent, and detailed information about their performance, and this is consistent with their prevalent "utility" orientation.

Note that messages emphasizing favorability and delivery characteristics did not negatively impact younger workers, nor did emphasis on the quality aspects negatively affect older workers – they just didn't matter much for those groups.

In this section we focused on feedback as an essential element of talent management for retention of employees of all ages. Feedback only goes so far, though, without the scaffolding of systematic career development strategies to provide a pathway to growth. It is a common assumption that career development is best directed toward younger and early career employees, but it is an integral and ongoing part of retaining strong employees across their lifespan. Read on for career development approaches to consider in your multi-age workforce.

Career Development

First, let's delineate how we're thinking about career development in the context of talent management across the lifespan. This can include the activities that are determined jointly by a manager and employee based on performance feedback to shore up any weak spots and to further capitalize on strengths. A host of activities[17,18] could be part of development, including:

- planned events such as training programs, conferences, seminars, and leader development programs;
- the arrangement or encouragement of developmental relationships, such as with mentors, coaches, career counselors, or networking groups;
- development work experiences on the job, including special and challenging assignments, job rotations, and task forces.

Note that we devoted another chapter to the many issues to consider in the design and implementation of training programs for employees across the lifespan (Chapter 4), so we do not focus on issues specific to training at this juncture.

Development can also be self-directed; employees are increasingly taking the wheel to manage their careers and may engage in self-development activities, ranging from reading and watching videos, to finding and enrolling in online courses on their own, to seeking out connections with others outside of the organization for guidance. Both organization-supported and self-directed development can be focused on specific growth and learning goals (e.g., become proficient at a new software program; develop strength in handling conflict), but these activities may also be used to manage an employee's long-term career trajectory.

New Tricks? Of Course!

Traditionally, development has been considered a younger person's game.[19] Perhaps there was a time when people climbed the organizational ladder and reached a point of mastery where they no longer needed to learn new skills, but that is certainly not the case now! However, conscious or unconscious stereotypes of older workers (as discussed in Chapter 6; e.g., uninterested and unable to learn new things, incompetent at new technologies, a poor future investment) may prevent managers from thinking of their older employees for new growth opportunities. Interestingly, even common positive stereotypes of older workers – that they are knowledgeable and experienced – may end up hurting them when they result in the impression that older workers don't need (or maybe even would scoff at) mentoring or coaching.[20] After all, the image of mentors is typically of older and wiser employees passing their advice on to the next generation. So, both positive and negative age stereotypes directly may feed into fewer opportunities for career development as employees age. In a worst-case scenario, this could leave an organization vulnerable to age discrimination claims if there is a pattern of older workers being adversely affected.[21] This can also lead to a vicious cycle whereby later-life employees may have lower self-efficacy (belief they can succeed) for growth and development and do not take the opportunities that do come along.

Self-efficacy has been shown to come from four possible sources (or combinations): actually mastering a task ("If I've done it before, I can do it again"), vicariously experiencing mastery by watching someone do it ("If she can do it, so can I"), persuasion ("My manager really thinks I've got what it takes to take on this new task force"), and physiological arousal ("I can feel that adrenaline pumping – let's do this thing!").

As employees age within an organization:

- they may get fewer opportunities to take on new things and master them.
- the people mastering new things don't look like them so don't seem like a good comparison group.
- managers may no longer think to encourage them to try new stuff, assuming they are happy where they are or uninterested.
- internalizing stereotypes and messages they receive may cause anxiety which may interfere with focus.

When self-efficacy is lowered, employees may volunteer for fewer opportunities or not persist through roadblocks or challenges that are bound to come with true learning experiences.[22]

Subjective Age and Future Time Remaining

The process of aging at work is obviously correlated with a person's chronological age.[23] However, as we have mentioned there is considerable variability in the aging process: People of the same age can have very different organizational behaviors, motivational levels, emotional needs, and health. Subjective age refers to factor such as how old a person says they *feel*, *act*, and *look*. Clearly, age management policies and interventions must not only address the person's chronological age but their subjective age as well.

An important, related explanation for why a person's motivation for developmental opportunities may decrease across the lifespan is that age is associated with what is called future time perspective (FTP), which we discussed briefly in Chapter 4.[24] Each of us tends to evaluate how much remaining time of his/her life is available to achieve significant goals, complete projects, develop new activities, and accept new challenges. Younger people, unsurprisingly, tend to have a more open-ended FTP (forgoing any health reasons to be more conscious of their mortality). In contrast, the older you are, the less available time you tend to estimate remaining (although this certainly happens at different rates for different people).

Occupational future time perspective (OFTP) refers specifically to worker's perception of remaining time and opportunities in their career.[25] OFTP has two aspects. The first, *remaining time*, gives an idea of the depth of the perspective over time (how many years I still see ahead of me at work). The second, *focus on opportunities*, gives an idea of the quality/intensity of the future time. For example, two workers, Ed and Kurt, are each five years out from retirement. Ed laments: "I have five years of routine ahead of me, with no prospects for growth. Boring!"; on the other hand, Kurt perceives the same time (five remaining years before retirement) as "full of new things, with opportunities to learn and fill new positions, and the potential of putting my experience to the service of others". Check out Special Focus Box 8.3 to see the types of questions that researchers interested in OFTP ask to assess it.

Indeed, recognizing differences in OFTP among workers can help us understand hesitation among some workers for participating in career

---

Special Focus Box 8.3: Survey Questions that Researchers Use to Estimate Occupational Future Time Perspective

A. *Perceived remaining time at work*
- Most of my occupational life lies ahead of me.
- My occupational future seems infinite to me.

B. *Focus on opportunities at work*
- My occupational future is filled with possibilities.
- Many opportunities await me in my occupational future.

---

development. For example, one study found that age differences in self-efficacy for learning and the value of learning could be *explained* by differences in FTP – this means that not age per se, but that age often corresponds to a more constrained FTP, that seems to account for why we may see less interest in development opportunities among older employees than younger.[26]

What Can Managers Do to Leverage OFTP?

There is some encouraging news here. Managers can use this information about obstacles to development opportunities to break these obstacles down and open doors. For example, all four avenues for building self-efficacy described above can open up when employees of all ages are supported through challenging assignments. Additionally, an environment that encourages continuous learning that suits individual needs and desires is more likely to be one where the fears of making mistakes are lessened as well.

Can OFTP Be Changed?

Future time perspective is also not set in stone. Helping late-career employees to access available opportunities could reduce their focus on losses and limits that can stifle motivation for development. A focus on opportunities is usually associated with job satisfaction, engagement, and a growth mindset. And there are ways in which work can increase focus on opportunities. For example, some job characteristics like job complexity are positively associated with this focus on opportunities. This means that exercising a highly complex work task can stimulate people's vitality and their psychological investment at work. Moreover, recent research showed that a positive *organizational climate for successful aging* (shared perceptions on organizational life and practices that facilitate successful aging at work) is able to reinforce older workers' focus on opportunities.[27] We will speak more of organizational-level factors that contribute to talent retention across the lifespan later in this chapter.

The Role of Leader as Coach

Taking on a coaching approach when leading employees regardless of age can enhance the continual feedback process.[28,29] It may be especially beneficial for older workers as it sends a message that the manager and by proxy the organization believe that people can grow and improve throughout their life. As always, keeping the lifespan development science in mind while not making assumptions about an employee because of their age is key. Any two 52-year-old employees may have different developmental needs, family constraints, work histories, and passions to take into account as they are encouraged and guided in their development. Talent is more likely to stay in a place where their uniqueness is appreciated.

What about When the Manager Is Younger Than the Employee?

People have often assumed an age-based social norm that defines the structuring of power roles in organizations. Traditionally, the assumption is that a team leader or a manager who leads a number of subordinates, or heads an organization, is older than their followers. Experience, knowledge, seniority, and prestige *legitimize* the position of the leader who assumes the role of guide for subordinates. But this social norm has been increasingly violated in more recent years. This emerging situation represents a sort of status incongruence, particularly for those older workers that consider themselves to be active and highly experienced; on some occasions this can undermine the authority of the leader and the effectiveness of the leader's action.

> **Special Focus Box 8.4: Younger Leaders and Older Employees**
>
> 1. *Win trust.* There could be awkwardness for both parties at the beginning. The ability to carefully and respectfully listen to and consider the experience of older employees must be the first resource to use to break potential mistrust and gain increasing levels of respect.
> 2. *Teamwork.* Building a positive and age-friendly group atmosphere. As outlined in Chapter 6, manage age perception in order to limit negative age stereotypes and give value to everyone's unique resources.
> 3. *Create opportunities.* As highlighted in the prior section, it is essential to offer professional development opportunities to people at all career stages, even the most advanced. These opportunities can encourage commitment and investment throughout the remaining career.

Having a much younger leader can make *some* older employees (not all, by any means) feel frustrated, producing negative reactions such as a loss of motivation and engagement. Such reactions, in turn, can have a negative impact on how the young leader assesses themselves as well as the performance and commitment of the senior employee. Under these conditions, a vicious cycle may occur – and the loss of two forms of talent might be at risk – the young leader and the older employee. This does not have to be the case. See Special Focus Box 8.4 for suggestions to avoid this chain of events.

Up until now we've largely discussed how individual managers/ leaders can take into account lifespan issues as they strive to retain their best talent. In the remainder of the chapter we perch at a higher level, focusing on how HR systems and practices within an organization can also be improved with an eye toward retaining talent over the life course of its employees.

Organizational-Level Approaches for Retaining Talent Across the Lifespan

We have discussed how the needs, motives, and expectancies may likely change for talented employees across their organizational lifespan (see Chapter 3). HR practices that recognize and account for these changes can be an important part of an organization-wide approach to retaining talent of all ages. And an underlying organization climate that values talent of all ages is key.

HR Strategies That Promote Different Workers

Some organizational decision-makers view older workers as a declining resource unworthy of further investment, or they view them as an important resource to be preserved and continually nurtured. From this point of view, the principles and vision of organizational strategies for human resources management are very important. A continuum can be identified to describe these strategies, from depreciation to conservation.[30] On one side are *depreciation* strategies, where older workers are considered as a diminishing resource for the organization, and late career is considered as a final step before the transition to retirement. This type of strategy communicates to older workers that they are no longer valued by the organization. The depreciation of older workers can lead to age-based discrimination in organizational decisions (selection, training, appraisal), marginalization of older workers, and their exclusion from responsibility, social networks, and decision-making processes. These organizational processes of devaluation of mature human resources also have consequences on individual motivation and confidence, on the perceived abilities and of self-efficacy ("I am not able any longer to do some part of my job"), and on the construction of negative self-stereotypes ("I am too old to carry out certain tasks and take on certain responsibilities that only younger worker can perform").

On the other side are *conservation* strategies, which consider older workers as an asset for the organization and support the late career of employees. Conservation strategies aim at more active management of late careers. Late careers are not considered a simple pre-exit phase, but as a phase with meaningful goals and opportunities for development. The HR strategies create a favorable organizational age-climate that sends workers a message of interest and respect from the organization. Conservation strategies help older worker to successfully adapt to their late career adaptation, giving them the opportunity to recognize personal strengths and to cope with career related setback.[31] Special Focus Box 8.5 provides a recent example of an intervention designed to enhance conservation strategies.

Special Focus Box 8.5: How to Enhance Thriving in Late Career

How can one orient one's organization toward conservation strategies? A worthy example is provided by an intervention aimed at *late career management preparedness*. Late-career management preparedness is when older workers are able and motivated to manage their late career and are also prepared to deal with career setbacks. A group of scientists from the Finnish Institute of Occupational Health recently tested an organizational intervention model evaluated by a randomized and controlled trial and confirmed the long-term positive effects of the intervention. The intervention consisted of workshops for older workers in different organizations. The intervention aimed to strengthen the readiness of late-career employees in three critical areas: (a) dealing with perceptions of age-based discrimination; (b) confidence in one's working skills; and (c) improvement of FTP at work.

The workshops were planned so that participants could actively participate by sharing their experiences with other colleagues. From this exchange of experiences, learning and awareness processes were activated, improving the workers' preparedness for career management. Here are some examples of the workshop content:

- Focus on *seniority skills*: how to highlight an employee's own skills and occupational experiences; how to share these experiences with colleagues;
- Promote *work ability* (or the ability to meet job requirements; see Chapter 5): how to manage one's own career during organizational changes; how to improve networking and social support;
- Strengthen *confidence in employability*: enhancing the opportunities for interesting new tasks.

The researchers found that:

a. the interventions were effective in strengthening late-career management preparedness;
b. the positive effects of the intervention continued after six months.
c. Those who participated in the workshops showed a wider occupational future time perspective and perceived less age discrimination at work compared with people that didn't participate at the workshops (control group).

Vuori, J., Törnroos, K., Ruokolainen, M., & Wallin, M. (2019). Enhancing late-career management among aging employees—A randomized controlled trial. *Journal of Vocational Behavior, 115.*

We know that human resource management practices are activities devoted to the management of people inside the organization that designed to increase worker productivity, positive organizational attitudes (organizational commitment, engagement, and identification), and well-being (satisfaction, physical health, and psychological health). Newer research suggests that the effects of such practices on these outcomes depend to some extent on workers' age, individual level of vitality, and career stage.[32] Although we most often hear the word "sustainability" in relation to the earth's environment, the term *Sustainable HR Practices* has been adopted by some to refer to those practices that allow for the maximal fit between workers and their environment over time and changing their life situations. The sustainability philosophy promotes decent work from a systems-based perspective, valuing resource preservation and regeneration, fairness, progress, and interconnectedness among members of the organization.[39] In addition, some approaches to sustainability focus on HR practices that are associated with *both* high performance of employees as well as their well-being.[33] This research shows that different HR practices will lead to both performance and well-being depending on the workers' age.

According to a study conducted on managers of several Dutch companies, different "bundles" of HR practices can be distinguished[34,35]:

- *Development*-oriented HR practices include career development, skills enhancement, and challenging assignments. They focus on advancement, growth, and accomplishment and that are functional for those people who want to achieve higher levels of success.
- *Maintenance*-oriented HR practices include less complex tasks and reduced responsibilities They are focused on protection, safety, and stability and that are more functional for those workers who want to maintain their position without taking risks or not accepting new challenges.
- *Utilization*-oriented HR practices include horizontal mobility and the progressive enrichment of tasks after a long absence due to injury or illness. They aim to recover and return to an earlier level of functioning after losing resources.
- *Accommodative* HR practices include reduced workload and partial or early retirement. They focus on allowing workers to operate adequately at lower levels of performance and suited to their resources and skills.

The use and effectiveness of these different bundles of HR practices depends in part on the age of the people involved. Generally speaking, the developmental bundle seems to produce more positive results for younger workers, while the maintenance bundle seems to work better among mature workers. But, the research conducted to date confirms that the effectiveness of these intervention strategies depends *not only* on the chronological age of the workers involved, *but also on the specific person's needs, motivations, and organizational investment.* Ultimately, high-involvement practices are aimed at promoting performance and job satisfaction for all workers. For example, some studies show that development practices tailored to older workers increase their intention to remain and be involved at work. These practices are interpreted as signals that the organization is interested in and takes care of workers of all ages, generating more job satisfaction and organizational commitment.[36] These strategies heighten performance and sustain well-being because they offer workers the chance to participate, have autonomy, and gain new skills. For these reasons, high involvement practices can buffer the resource losses that may come with aging and can slow performance declines in late career.

The Secret Sauce: Organizational Climate (and the Role of HR in Fostering It)

A top-management philosophy of retaining and nurturing talent through their life stages is essential, as are the high-impact HR policies and practices that support this philosophy. But there is one last element for us to consider in this chapter: do employees of the organization, from top to bottom and from start to finish, truly believe that the organization is age-friendly? And, does each employee's identification and psychological sense of membership to the organization maintain or even grow over the course of their life with the company and the changes the life course and career course brings?

Researchers have tried to understand how to support a good age climate in organizations and why that matters. In fact, the research in this area is compelling. For example, Boehm and colleagues did a large study on the age diversity climate (whether employees felt that people were supported regardless of their age) of 93 companies and totaling 14,260 employees. They found that having age-inclusive HR practices – like age-neutral recruiting, equal access to training, equal promotion opportunities, training managers on how to support people of different ages, and the promotion of a positive age culture – affected the organization's age diversity climate, and that the age diversity climate led to company performance and whether employees desired to stay with the company. In other words, the age diversity climate is key to company performance, and the lever available to organizations to improve the age diversity climate is HR practices that are beneficial to *all* workers regardless of their age.[37]

Another perspective on age climate is the *organizational climate for successful aging* (OCSA), or the shared perception that the organization appreciates workers of all ages.[38] See Special Focus Box 8.6 for some

---

Special Focus Box 8.6: Does Your Organization Have a Good Climate Regarding Employee Age?

A Good Age Diversity Climate?

How strongly do your employees agree with these statements?

1. Our company makes it easy for people from diverse age groups to fit in and be accepted.
2. Where I work, employees are developed and advanced without regard to the age of the individual.
3. Managers in our company demonstrate through their actions that they want to hire and retain an age-diverse workforce.
4. I feel that my immediate manager/supervisor does a good job of managing people with diverse backgrounds (in terms of age).

A Good Climate for Successful Aging?

How strongly do your employees agree with these statements?

1. Our company is aware of changes that take place with increasing employee age.
2. Our company takes age-related changes in employees' personal circumstances (e.g., family or care responsibilities) into account.
3. Our company is equally supportive of employees from different age groups.

Boehm, S. A., Kunze, F., & Bruch, H. (2014). Spotlight on age-diversity climate: The impact of age-inclusive HR practices on firm-level outcomes. *Personnel Psychology, 67*, 667–704.

questions for assessing this in your organization. This perspective gets at whether people believe that the organization not only appreciates all age groups but takes into account circumstances likely to arrive at different life stages. If this perception is not shared widely among organization members, it could mean that the organization has some work to do in terms of what their HR practices actually are, or it could mean that these values and resultant practices are not being communicated well to employees.

The onboarding process, where new employees learn the ropes of their job and the ins and outs of the organization, is also when the organization's values begin to emerge.[39] It could be through what those who manage and assist in this process, either formally or informally, are actually saying and doing directly, or what new folks pick up on more subtly. For example, is youth-centered language being used to describe good performance? Are people of all ages represented as key members of the organization? There are a lot of ways messages are sent; are the messages consistently communicating strong messages of support of age diversity?

There are many reasons why good talent leaves an organization, and there is no magic potion that will prevent it. But, in addition to the obvious – competitive compensation and benefits – cultivating a true sense of organizational membership where part of employee's identity includes their role in the organization can help. This sense of inclusion derives from three main things. A person should feel that their needs are fulfilled, they matter to people in the organization, and that they are an insider.[40]

Armstrong-Stasser and Schlosser, two Canadian researchers, found that the organization and managers can work together to help older workers maintain this sense of inclusion. In summing up their findings, they state that "Older workers will want to remain a member of their organization when their organization engages in practices tailored to the needs of older workers, their supervisor implements these practices fairly, and their organization conveys that it values the contribution of its older workers thereby fostering a strong sense of belonging" (p. 319).[41] A truly age-friendly environment will ensure this sense of inclusion is fostered for employees of all ages, and is sustained over time as they age.

Eventually, of course, there will be a time where members of your valued older workforce do retire. Ensuring that their specialized knowledge is respected, appropriately captured, and passed on in the organization is vital; see Special Focus Box 8.7 for an example of an organization creating technology to preserve and transfer important knowledge in a way that doesn't burden your departing employees but preserves their valued knowledge for others.

Special Focus Box 8.7: New Ways to Transfer Knowledge: A Case Study

An issue that arises when discussing the aging workforce with organizational policy-makers is the challenge of retaining knowledge when a person retires. This includes not only job knowledge, but also implicit knowledge about how to get things done that is often not captured in manuals. For example, whom do you go to if you have a question about billing? The current research on how to manage this transfer of knowledge suggests that organizations can support knowledge transfer across generations by using age-inclusive HR practices and supporting a positive age-diversity climate. In addition, some organizations hire back retirees for short periods, or even informally call retirees with questions when the need arises. However, more systematic, technological solutions may be developing as well. Here we provide an example.

Richard Weiher and Armin Müller von Fischer of KnowKit Solutions (https://knowkit.com) have developed a knowledge transfer solution. It was originally conceptualized as a way to support knowledge transfer to new hires. But it can also be framed from the retirement viewpoint: How to pass along the knowledge and wisdom of older workers to junior colleagues.

They came upon their idea because they found that many new employees tend to ask the same questions multiple times as they are coming onboard. Traditionally, organizations have addressed this issue by developing detailed manuals. Such manuals were cumbersome to develop and equally difficult to use. Weiher and von Fischer's idea was to find a technological solution for capturing employee knowledge. Based on client input, they developed a system where an employee is recorded while doing their job, for as briefly as an hour to as long as a couple of weeks. This could be a video of the employee, or possibly a recording capturing the work being done on the employee's computer. It is also helpful if the employee uses a "think aloud" approach as they move through their work; that is, they explain what they are doing and why. For example, an employee might explain, "I'm going to the field in the upper right of my screen which contains a dropdown menu of approved vendors". (This process of observing the employee would obviously need to be approved by the employee due to privacy issues.)

The key to their technology is its searchability. A new employee simply puts questions into a search engine that finds possible text or sections of video where the answer might be. That is, the technology searches over hours or weeks of employee recordings and to find the answer to new employees' questions, showing the part of the recording with the answer.

For example, a senior employee who manages warehouse processes has been recorded at their job for a period of two weeks. In the recordings, they talk about the steps involved in their job, with the details and challenges about how to move materials from one warehouse to another – including contextual details that are impossible to cover in a manual. The recording has also included shots of their computer screen as they use it to move through their job tasks. Later, a new employee might ask the search engine, "How do I move things from one warehouse to another?" They would then be shown the 10 minutes of video – among many hours' worth – where the senior employee explains how to do that. Such a description would also likely include the "tacit knowledge" that is never covered in a manual.

One added benefit of this approach is that for senior employees, the process can act as a diary that allows them to examine their current processes and possible ways to improve them. And more importantly, they don't need to be asked the same questions by 5 junior people. Weiher and von Fischer note, "From the experienced employee's perspective, it frees them from the burden of filling in everyone because they may be the only person with that information. This software solves that problem so that many people have the information".

There are some challenges to using this approach. Obviously, not all employees will want to be recorded in this way, or they may find it threatening. However, Weiher and von Fischer find that many organizations like the system as it has the added benefit of finding weaknesses in current practices and areas for improvement. This is especially the case for high-performance teams. For instance, it may be that the current process for moving material among warehouses could be streamlined, and this process would uncover ways to improve the system.

In any case, this example shows the possibility of using technological solutions to help preserve the organizational knowledge of high-performing, valuable employees.

Burmeister, A., van der Heijden, B., Yang, J., & Deller, J. (2018). Knowledge transfer in age-diverse coworker dyads in China and Germany: How and when do age-inclusive human resource practices have an effect? *Human Resource Management Journal, 28*(4), 605–620.

Burmeister, A., & Deller, J. (2016). Knowledge retention from older and retiring workers: What do we know, and where do we go from here? *Work, Aging and Retirement, 2*(2), 87–104.

The PIERA Approach to Late-Career Development

Some of the ideas that emerged in this chapter can be rethought in terms of interventions, following the PIERA model. We propose that you to think about how things work in your organization or within your work team and to adjust and tailor the ideas that we suggest below.

Planning

- *Organizational demography.* What is the organizational demography within your organization or team? How many people, in absolute and percentage terms, are in a late-career phase (say the last 10 years before retirement)? What organizational seniority do they have? What positions of responsibility do they occupy?
- *Status incongruence*: Are there older people in late career that can experience a status incongruence situation? Are there situations of young leaders and managers who guide older people? Can forms of discomfort and motivational failure linked to this inconsistency be detected?
- *Future time perspective.* It is appropriate to estimate, through individual interviews (or questionnaires in the case of large numbers), what the OFTP of people in the late career is. In this way it may be possible to estimate the starting potential on which the interventions will rest.
- *Constitution of heterogeneous groups.* Based on the previous points, is it possible to focus attention on well-defined types of workers in the late career in terms of career position, occupational time perspective, and readiness to manage late career. This diagnostic part allows you to plan awareness-raising training interventions that include workers with different characteristics.
- *Age culture and climate.* Examine what the age climate in your organization. Have age management interventions already been implemented in your organization? Can you say that your organization implements interventions and HR practices to encourage the retention and enhancement of workers of all ages? Do you think that in your organization there is a positive climate (within the working groups) accepting of age differences?

Implementation

- *Content.* The intervention can retrace what is described in Special Focus Box 8.5. Topics related to skills possessed, the value of seniority in organizations, the professional potential in the late career, the opportunities to enrich working position can be discussed inside the groups.
- *Structure.* Heterogeneous groups, made up of 8–12 people in the late career, can be created. Within the groups a facilitator (with organizational

psychology or similar background, if possible) can promote the exchange of experiences between the participants.

- *Purpose.* The positive experiences and motivational boost of people with greater ability to manage their late career should inspire even the least pro-active workers who start with a more limited occupational time perspective and with "downward" employment projections. The presence of a facilitator can also encourage discussion on some experiences of professional discomfort, especially in relation to supervisors, and on ways to approach them.

Evaluation

- *Monitoring.* During the course of the work, feedback can be requested from the participants to understand to what extent they appreciate the intervention and consider it useful in order to strengthen the active planning of the late career.
- *Counseling.* The facilitator can give some feed-back about the topics discussed during the group activities.
- *Assessment.* During the two months following the intervention, a series of data and information by the late career workers involved can be gathered: (a) productivity; (b) organizational commitment; (c) organizational citizenship behavior; (d) proposals for adjusting and improving their design of and approach to their task and duties.

Reflection

- *Data analysis.* Once the data are collected, you should look for trends. Do the data mirror the purpose of the intervention? Where are there inconsistencies? Is anything jumping out at you as particularly successful or problematic? In this way, you can estimate the impact of the initiative. Obviously, to fully estimate the effect of the intervention it would be desirable to have a control group that, in the same period of time, does not carry out the intervention. But such experimental designs are usually difficult to implement in organizations; it is still worthwhile to implement on a small scale without these controls, realizing the limitations to the firmness of conclusions.

Adjustment

- *Involvement of the participants.* A reflection on the outcomes of the intervention (positive or negative; expected or unexpected) can be conducted directly with the participants in the intervention after 4–6 months. In this way it is possible to estimate how long-lasting the effects of the intervention are and what corrective measures to introduce in future initiatives.

**Action Items: Things to Do Right Now,
Next Week, and Long Term…**

Things to Do Right Now

Skim back over the chapter and any notes you took. Did anything jump out at you as something you hadn't thought about before when you've considered retention strategies? Which points deserve further consideration for your own team? Write those down.

Things to Do Next Week

Think about some of the people on your team who have been there a while. Do you have a good idea what their career goals are right now? Have you noted how they may have changed over time? Can you find some time next week to schedule any needed one-on-ones with members of your team to check in to see how interests and goals may be shifting and to think about what types of development opportunities might be most relevant for those team members?

Things to Do Long Term

Are you aware of whether your organization's approach to HR policies for senior employees takes more of a deprecation or conservation approach? Even if HR touts a conservation approach, is this evident to the older workers in the organization? Can you think of ways to communicate the benefits of moving toward the conservation side of the continuum (if needed) and communicating it to employees? Who can help with this?

Notes

1. Nijs, S., Gallardo-Gallardo, E., Dries, N., Sels, L., & Leuven, K. (2014). A multidisciplinary review into the definition, operationalization, and measurement of talent. *Journal of World Business, 49*, 180–191.
2. Lee, G. (2018). Talent measurement: A holistic model and routes forward. *South African Journal of Human Resource Management, 16.* https://doi.org/10.4102/sajhrm.v16i0.990
3. Church, A. H., & Rotolo, C. T. (2013). How are top companies assessing their high-potentials and senior executives? A talent management benchmark study. *Consulting Psychology Journal: Practice and Research, 65*, 199–223.

4. Eurich, T. L., Krause, D. E., Cigularov, K., & Thornton, G. C. (2009). Assessment Centers: Current practices in the United States. *Journal of Business and Psychology, 24,* 387–407.

5. Finkelstein, L. F., Costanza, D. P., & Goodwin, G. (2018). Do your high potentials have potential? The impact of individual differences and designation on leader success. *Personnel Psychology, 71,* 3–22.

6. Klein, R. M., Dilchert, S., Ones, D. S., & Dages, K. D. (2015). Cognitive predictors and age-based adverse impact among business executives. *Journal of Applied Psychology, 100,* 1497–1510.

7. Mulligan, C., & Taylor, C. (2019). *Talent keepers: How top leaders engage and retain their best performers.* Hoboken, NJ: Wiley.

8. Stone, D., & Heen, S. (2014). *Thanks for the feedback: The science and art of receiving feedback well* (p. 4). New York, NY: Penguin Books.

9. Stone and Heen (2014).

10. Dello Russo, S., Miraglia, M., & Borgogni, L. (2016). Reducing organizational politics in performance appraisal: The role of coaching leaders for age-diverse employees. *Human Resource Management, 56,* 769–783.

11. Pichler, S. Beenen, G., & Wood, S. (2018). Feedback frequency and appraisal reactions: A meta-analytic test of moderators. *The International Journal of Human Resource Management, 31,* 2238–2263. https://doi.org/10.1080/09585 192.2018.1443961

12. Chawla, N., Gabriel, A. S., Dahling, J. J., & Patel, K. (2016). Feedback dynamics are critical to improving performance management systems. *Industrial and Organizational Psychology, 9,* 260–266.

13. Pichler, S. (2012). The social context of performance appraisal and appraisal reactions: A meta-analysis. *Human Resource Management, 51,* 709–732.

14. Sherf and Morrison (2020).

15. Correll, S., & Simard, C. (2016). *Research: Vague feedback is holding women back.* HBR.org. April 29, 2016.

16. Wang, M., Burlacu, G., Truxillo, D., James, K., & Yao, X. (2015). Age differences in feedback reactions: The roles of employee feedback orientation on social awareness and utility. *Journal of Applied Psychology, 100,* 1296–1308.

17. Maurer, T. J. (2001). Career-relevant learning and development, work age, and beliefs about self-efficacy for development. *Journal of Management, 27,* 123–140.

18. King, E. B., Botsford, W., Hebl, M. R., Kazama, S., & Dawson, J. F. (2012). Benevolent sexism at work: Gender differences in the distribution of challenging developmental experiences. *Journal of Management, 38,* 1835–1866.

19. Maurer, T. J., & Rafuse, N. E. (2001. Learning, not litigating: Managing employee development and avoiding claims of age discrimination. *Academy of Management Perspectives, 15*, 110–121.

20. Finkelstein, L. M., Allen, T. D., & Rhoton, L. A. (2003). An examination of the role of age in mentoring relationships. *Group and Organization Management, 28*, 249–281.

21. Maurer and Refuse (2001).

22. Maurer (2001).

23. Nagy, N., Johnston, C. S., & Hirschi, A. (2019) Do we act as old as we feel? An examination of subjective age and job crafting behaviour of late career employees. *European Journal of Work and Organizational Psychology, 28(3)*, 373–383.

24. Kochoian, N., Raemdonk, I., Frenay, M., & Zacher, H. (2017). The role of age and occupational future time perspectives in workers' motivation to learn. *Vocations and Learning, 10*, 27–45.

25. Henry, H., Zacher, H., & Desmette, D. (2017). Future time perspective in the work context: A systematic review of quantitative studies. *Frontiers in Psychology, 8*, 413. https://doi.org/10.3389/fpsyg.2017.00413

26. Zacher, H., & Frese, M. (2009). Remaining time and opportunities at work: Relationships between age, work characteristics, and occupational future time perspective. *Psychology and Aging, 24*, 487–493.

27. Zacher, H., & Yang, J. (2016). Organizational climate for successful aging. *Frontiers in Psychology, 7*. https://doi.org/10.3389/fpsyg.2016.01007

28. Chawla et al. (2016).

29. Della Russo et al. (2016).

30. Kooij, D. T. A. M., & Van De Voorde, K. (2015). Strategic HRM for older workers. In P. M. Bal, D. T. A. M. Kooij, & D. M. Rousseau (Eds.), *Aging workers and the employee-employer relationship* (pp. 57–72). Dordrecht: Springer.

31. Rudolph, C., Lavigne, K., & Zacher, H. (2017). Career adaptability: A meta-analysis of relationships with measures of adaptivity, adapting responses, and adaptation results. *Journal of Vocational Behavior, 98*, 17–34.

32. Innocenti, L., Profili, S., & Sammarra, A. (2013). Age as a moderator in the relationship between HR development practices and employee positive attitudes. *Personnel Review, 42*, 724–744.

33. Tordera, N., Peiró, J. M., Ayala, N., Villajos, E., & Truxillo, D. M. (2020). The lagged influence of organizations' human resources practices on employees' career sustainability: The moderating role of age. *Journal of Vocational Behavior, 20*.

34. de Lange, A. H., Kooij, D. T., & van der Heijden, B. I. (2015). Human resource management and sustainability at work across the lifespan: An integrative perspective. In L. M. Finkelstein, D. M. Truxillo, F. Fraccaroli, & R. Kanfer (Eds.). *Facing the challenges of a multi-age workforce: A use-inspired approach* (pp. 50–80). New York: Routledge.

35. Kooij, D. T. A. M., Jansen, P. G. W., Dikkers, J. S. E., & de Lange, A. H. (2014). Managing aging employees: A mixed methods study on bundles of HR practices for aging employees. *The International Journal of Human Resource Management, 25*, 2192–2212.

36. Kooij, D. T. A. M., Guest, D., Clinton, M., Knight, T., Jansen, P. G. W., & Dikkers, J. S. E. (2013). How the impact of HR practices on employee well-being and performance changes with age. *Human Resource Management Journal, 23*(1), 18–35.

37. Boehm, S. A., Kunze, F., & Bruch, H. (2014). Spotlight on age-diversity climate: The impact of age-inclusive HR practices on firm-level outcomes. *Personnel Psychology, 67*, 667–704.

38. Zacher and Yang (2016).

39. Ashforth, B. E., Sluss, D. M., & Harrison, S. H. (2007). Socialization in organizational contexts. In G. P. Hodgkinson & J. K. Ford (Eds.), *International review of industrial and organizational psychology* (Vol. 22, pp. 1–70).

40. Masterson, S. S., & Stamper, C. L. (2003). Perceived organizational membership: An aggregate framework representing the employee-organization relationship. *Journal of Organizational Behavior, 24*, 473–490.

41. Armstrong-Stassen, M., & Schlosser, F. (2011). Perceived organizational membership and the retention of older workers. *Journal of Organizational Behavior, 32*, 319–344.

Keeping up the Good Work

9

Self-Managed Coaching with PIERA

Employees learn from each other and their leaders. The success of creating a PIERA culture in your unit depends on whether you are able to adopt and model this approach to issues you confront in your own work life. Previous chapters have described in detail how managers can use PIERA to help their employees improve work-life balance, improve team inclusivity, and so on. This chapter extends that discussion one step further by focusing on how **you** can develop effective self-coaching skills to enhance personal and professional development in yourself and, by extension others you manage.

As we have emphasized, people encounter challenges that may affect their productivity and well-being throughout their careers. During mid- and late-career, these challenges may affect your self-confidence and work attitudes. Ageism, lack of supervisory support, boredom, demands for learning new skills, and feelings of social isolation are just some of the situations that can lead to negative feelings toward one's job and thoughts of early retirement. Drawing from the self-management literature, the PIERA approach outlined in Figure 9.1, depicts the process through which people have the potential for being their own coach – that is, for taking charge and managing their thoughts, behaviors, and environment in ways that can contribute to a more satisfying and successful work life.

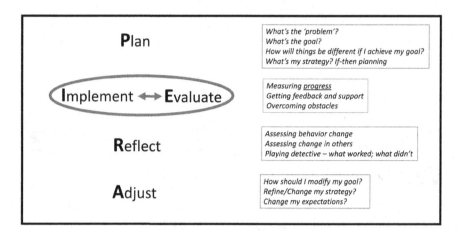

Plan

What's the 'problem'?
What's the goal?
How will things be different if I achieve my goal?
What's my strategy? If-then planning

Implement ⟷ **E**valuate

Measuring _progress_
Getting feedback and support
Overcoming obstacles

Reflect

Assessing behavior change
Assessing change in others
Playing detective – what worked; what didn't

Adjust

How should I modify my goal?
Refine/Change my strategy?
Change my expectations?

Figure 9.1   Making PIERA work for you

Noticing a Problem: Is My Job Still a Good Fit?

You can't plan a solution without knowing what the problem is and setting a goal to address it. Several years ago, one of the authors received a call from a mid-career level senior human resource manager asking for help in making a job change. "Yolanda" indicated that she was bored with her job and felt she was treated disrespectfully by the younger managers in her office. After some discussion it became clear that Yolanda did not really want to change her job or her career, but simply didn't know any other way to improve her situation. For many mid-career workers with relatively long company tenure, work role problems and interpersonal differences can simmer for a long time before becoming problematic. Sometimes specific events can set off strong feelings of work discomfort. For example, the recent pandemic required many educators and employees to rapidly learn new IT skills in order to perform their job. Among late career employees who lacked confidence in their learning abilities relative to younger coworkers, this event may have led to thoughts of retirement. Whether the cause of discomfort has developed slowly or in response to a specific event, people often think that the only way to fix a work problem is to find other work or to retire. In many cases, however, a PIERA approach can be used to develop a less radical and more satisfying solution. _Noticing a problem in how you think or feel about your work and the people you work with_ is the first step in activating a PIERA solution.

Bounding the Problem and Setting a Goal

Many emerging challenges in mid- and late-career arise from *change* – in you, the organization, or both. One of the most important steps for preparing yourself to use PIERA is to identify what that change is and how it relates to the difficulty and discomfort you are experiencing. For example, increasing stress associated with work-nonwork conflict may be traced to a new supervisor who appears less supportive of your flexible work schedule. Alternatively, you may feel bored at work performing the same tasks you have for years. Or you might find yourself feeling less connected to new, younger members of your work team. Although these problems may not directly affect your job performance, a PIERA approach may reduce your stress and renew your enjoyment at work.

As you may recall from Chapter 3, research findings show that the goals and strategies people use when confronting problems are often subtly influenced by age-related gains and losses.[1] During young adulthood, people tend to adopt goals that focus on *gains*, such as taking on a difficult project, that maximize opportunities for achievement and promotion. In contrast, during mid- and later-adulthood, people begin to shift toward adoption of goals that *optimize* previous gains (e.g., apply the skills that they have gained through prior work) or, in later years, *compensate* for age-related losses in abilities (de-emphasize things they can't do anymore while applying skills they are best at). These kinds of goals might involve crafting your job tasks with your supervisor to allow you to utilize your strongest work talents, or arranging your work schedule to allow you to take care of nonwork needs. Although the problem you identify in the fit between you and your work may call for a gain-based goal (e.g., learning a new technology; building rapport with younger workers), other concerns might call for formulating an optimization goal (e.g., increasing mentoring activities) or a compensatory goal (e.g., performing fewer physically-demanding tasks; increasing the variety of tasks you perform on your job). People can use a variety of strategies (e.g., job crafting) to cope with a problem, but you must first know your goal – what is it you want to be different?

Goals are our desired outcome states. Goals are not limited to fixing problems (such as work-life imbalance); sometimes people set goals to achieve something new (e.g., create a new program), improve their well-being (e.g., become more physically fit), or further develop their skills (e.g., time management). Regardless of whether you goal is to resolve a problem or develop yourself, it is important to reflect on how your life and work will be different if you accomplish your goal. For example, you might have a declining parent whose care is demanding more time than you expected. Although you don't have to provide direct care-giving, it takes time during business hours to talk with doctors, arrange appointments, pay bills, and deal with other challenges. Your initial thought is to set a goal that gives you one day off per week. But after some reflection, you might realize that such a goal would not fully meet your needs, and you might still need to respond to caregivers during other weekdays. Before setting this goal to address this concern, you want to consider the nature of the caregiving demands, when they occur, and much time they typically take. Maybe arranging a flexible schedule would be a better goal, so that you could deal with your parent's needs when they arise. The point here is that goals are powerful mental guides in our life and should only be undertaken when we truly believe that achieving the goal will improve our life.

To be effective you must reflect before you commit to a goal. Consider how much your work and life situation will be different (What will be better? What will not change? What might be worse?) if you achieve your goal. Ask yourself: "Am I willing and able to devote energy to accomplishing this goal at this time?" How important is this goal? If I accomplish the goal, how would my work life be better? How much is this goal under my control? That is, even if I put in a lot of effort, is the outcome something that I can influence or help make to happen? And would things be improved even if I partially accomplished my goal? If you cannot foresee any improvement in your situation with even partial goal progress, you may need to rethink your goal.

It is also important to remember that some problems, particularly those involving interpersonal conflicts and disrespectful treatment from others, cannot not be completely "fixed" or eliminated entirely. Think about what actions by others are most uncomfortable or upsetting to you. Focus on what proactive and/or preventive strategies you can use to reduce the likelihood of experiencing these hurtful behaviors. Remember Yolanda, from earlier in the chapter? She might develop a set of proactive responses that aim to reduce the frequency of disrespectful comments. For example, she could say "I understand what you are saying, but I hope you understand that the way you said it to me was hurtful. I can hear your concern much better when you do not tell me in a hurtful way".

Finally, it is important to remember that goals must be realistic and within your grasp to achieve, albeit with some effort, planning, and practice. For example, if the problem is simply "your manager", it would be

Special Focus Box 9.1: Set a Goal Exercise

Identify and write down three specific work-related goals for yourself.

1. _____
2. _____
3. _____

Evaluate each goal with the following questions:

1. Is this goal SMART (Specific, Measurable, Achievable, Relevant, Time-bound)?
2. Will achieving this goal part or wholly relieve my discomfort with my work or accomplish my desire?
3. Is this a goal under my control? How much effort on my part is needed to accomplish this goal? (rate on 1–10 scale: (1) hardly any effort, (10) all my effort).
4. All things considered, is this goal worth the effort?

unrealistic to set a goal of getting a new manager unless you are planning to transfer or quit. Use the goal setting exercise in Special Focus Box 9.1 to identify outcome states that you believe **your** actions can positively influence.

Researchers investigating factors that affect goal success repeatedly find that clearly describing and reflecting on your goal, as you did in the exercise above, is a critical step in changing behavior and the future.[2] The exercise helps you to concretize your goals and decide whether it is feasible to elevate a wish or desire to the level of an actionable goal. Spending time to specify and refine your goal helps you understand your wishes better and ultimately adopt a more realistic goal. Once you have clarified your goal, the next step is to make a plan.

Building a Successful Plan: Strategies and If/Then Planning

Some goals can be accomplished without generating a strategy, such as checking your inbox. But many important life goals require a plan. Plans are more than general strategies; research shows that achieving your goal requires two additional features.[3] First, you must think about possible strategies and identify the one that is most likely to achieve success. Second, you must identify potential obstacles in this strategy and plan what you will do if those obstacles materialize. This is called "if/then" planning. Research findings show that people who consciously and purposively develop if/then solutions for challenges they may encounter along the way have significantly greater success attaining their goal than those who don't. For example, your goal may be to improve your listening skills with your subordinates. When do you tend to get distracted? What small thing can you do to keep yourself engaged in the conversation? How can you "stay in the moment?" If strategies provide the blueprint for how to achieve your goal, if/then plans are the tactics by which you can stay on course. Be sure to arm yourself with enough if/then tactics for the challenges you are likely to face.

Selecting a strategy can be daunting. Goals that involve self-improvement such as increasing one's fitness or learning a new technology are often a matter of reworking your schedule to allow for the activity. For many people, the problem is not scheduling, but rather overcoming internal obstacles to *doing* the activity, such as not feeling up to the activity or not wanting to quit what you are currently doing. If/then plans that include public commitments to colleagues, friends, to instructors and so on, increase the likelihood that you will follow through on your plan. Engaging in activities with others (e.g., enrolling in a technology course with a colleague) is another way of shoring up your commitment.

Strategies to accomplish relationship-change goals (e.g., to improve your relationship with your subordinates) are more complicated. Strategies for these goals are often difficult to initiate and often take longer to accomplish. Changing a relationship involves not only changing your behavior, but having the other person recognize and respond to that change. Understandably, people may not immediately respond to you in the way that you would like. Among older adults, initiating conversations with younger workers may be intimidating, and you may feel that you have little in common for casual conversations. Enlist the assistance of your colleagues to help you identify differences between you and your younger employees or coworkers in language used, communication patterns, and potential topics of mutual interest. Try out new ways of connecting and keep at it until the younger employee recognizes that your behavior is not an accident but an overture for relationship change. These strategies are also useful for younger people who may not know how to approach their older colleagues or subordinates.

Special Focus Box 9.2: Generate a Strategy and If/Then Plans

GOAL: _____

My strategy to accomplish the goal is: _____

Identify 3 likely obstacles you will confront as you implement your strategy. Indicate exactly what you will do if they occur to overcome them.

Obstacle: _____

How I will overcome the obstacle: _____

_____

Obstacle: _____

How I will overcome the obstacle: _____

_____

Obstacle: _____

How I will overcome the obstacle: _____

_____

Use the worksheet in Special Focus Box. 9.2 to practice self-reflection on strategy development and if/then planning. Select one goal from Special Focus Box 9.1. For that goal, indicate the strategy you plan to adopt, and three potential obstacles or problems along with your plan to deal with them.

Goal Pursuit: Putting Your Plan into Action and Measuring Your Progress

Once you have reflected on your goal, formulated a strategy, and addressed potential obstacles, you are almost ready to put your plan into action! Before you begin, however, you must build in performance/progress markers by which to measure how well you are doing. Measures of your performance or goal progress provide feedback that allows you to fairly evaluate your progress and make adjustments to your plan if necessary. Performance/progress markers can also boost your motivation. In the absence of performance indicators, people often make under- and over-estimates of their progress – estimates that reduce effort just when more effort may be needed!

When learning a new technology, for example, going by your "sense" of how you are doing might discourage you when in fact you are making good progress. In this example, you can use self-tests or time to complete a task with the new technology as an indicator of your learning progress. The good feeling that you get when you do well on a self-test can provide just enough motivation to push you forward. If you don't do as well as expected, you can think about ways to adjust your strategy and effort for the next round. If your goal is to improve work-life balance by changing your schedule, you can create weekly indicators of how successfully you managed your schedule over the week and the number of days you encountered work-life conflicts. If you find that you have difficulty making your planned schedule change week after week, it is time to pause and think about the nature of the obstacles you're facing and alternative strategies that might be more successful.

Measures of goal progress come in many forms, each with its own advantages and disadvantages. Depending on your goal, you might use a count measure or some other quantitative indicator of daily or weekly behaviors. These are often the easiest to obtain and you can do this yourself by keeping a performance diary. However, it is important to make use of other indicators of progress as well. One such indicator is the feedback you get from colleagues or friends. Such feedback may be in the form of a compliment or just a statement indicating a noticed change in your behavior. Researchers have found that experienced workers are less likely to ask colleagues for feedback on how they are doing than less experienced employees.[4] However, if you are comfortable sharing your goal project with others, you can enlist them to help you evaluate your progress, particularly when it involves relationship change. Others can also provide motivation in the form of emotional support during goal pursuit.

A third, often neglected form of feedback comes from listening to your own bodily and emotional reactions to your goal effort and progress. There is growing evidence that goal progress is associated with feelings of pride, positive affect, and a sense of well-being.[5] Listening to your own thoughts and feelings can also be useful in evaluating whether your strategy needs tweaking.

What kind of performance information or feedback should you seek? In general, researchers have found that the most useful markers and feedback change as you move closer to your goal.[6] Early in goal pursuit, the more effective feedback and markers tend to be those that indicate *how far you have come* from beginning your project. If your goal is to improve your food choices, then you want to compare your daily choice behavior to what you were doing before you began pursuing your goal – *not* how far you have to go in order to meet your goal. The adage "Rome wasn't built in a day" is meant for you at this point – goal accomplishment takes time! In contrast, as you close in on your goal, research findings suggest that it is motivating to evaluate your progress in terms of your final goal; that is, *how close are you to accomplishing your goal?*

Reflection

All goal pursuits end. Sometimes we meet our goal and turn to other pursuits. Other times we experience overwhelming obstacles that prompt us to give up on our goal. More often, however, we adjust our goal to one that is within our reach. Regardless of how your goal pursuit unfolds, this is *not* the end of the PIERA process. *Arguably one of the most valuable parts of the PIERA process is the reflection and adjustment that takes place either during a pause or at the end of a goal pursuit.* Reflection is much like a debriefing after a military operation or a surgical procedure. During reflection you have an opportunity to review the entire episode and think about what went right, what went wrong, what strategies worked best, and how well you did in coping with planned and unplanned obstacles. In contrast to the reflection that is done during the "hot" period of goal pursuit, reflection at the end of an episode gives you an opportunity to see the big picture with respect to the effectiveness of your strategies and how you feel about the goal.

Adjustment

As you reflect on the goal pursuit process, you will learn more about yourself and your situation. This learning can be invaluable for identifying future work and career goals. For example, we know that person-job fit is an important determinant of job satisfaction. Among long-tenured leaders and managers, successful aging in the workplace requires regular updating of the job to maximize person-job fit. During the early years of adulthood, new learning opportunities typically abound. As employees advance and age, however, new work-related learning opportunities are often less common. In concert with age-related changes in motives and the introduction of new technologies that change job demands, the job may start to feel stale or overwhelming. In essence, the person-job fit that was present when you first began your career may be out of whack. The adjustment phase refers to working through how you can realign your needs and competencies with the demands of the job.

For example, one of us recently worked with a woman in her 50s, we'll call Betty, who was employed in the Human Resources Division as a trainer in a very large technology company. Although she was a high performer and valued by her supervisor and colleagues, she felt increasingly less engaged in her work. The introduction of new training technologies over the past few years required her to spend much of her day learning new technology skills and to perform administrative work, resulting in less in-course time actually training employees. She talked with her supervisor about how to craft the job to give her more time working with trainees, but her boss had few suggestions for how she might spend more time training. After a few months, Betty decided to seek new employment that would provide a better fit to her skills and goals. Her strategy was to network with other trainers outside her firm and to pursue openings as they arose. She decided to give her job search effort a year and then to reflect on her progress.

During her job search, Betty met people working independently, in small businesses, and in other large firms. She applied to several positions and sought feedback from friends and family about how to market her skills. After about nine months with no new job success, she paused to reflect and adjust her goal. She realized that large firms were more interested in applicants with more extensive technology background. Further, she noticed that the positions available entailed more travel than was possible given her nonwork demands. As a consequence of her reflection and discussion with her family, she decided to adjust her work goal – to become an independent sales training consultant. She developed a strategy and identified a set of milestones in her goal pursuit. With this new goal in place, Betty spoke with her supervisor about crafting a bridge job that would provide her time to develop her business and allow her to retire from the company with maximum benefits. Six months before her bridge term ended, she established her company and began seeking business. Although there were certainly bumps in the road to her goal, she is currently self-employed doing work that she enjoys and that utilizes her strongest competencies.

Of course not every career transition goes so smoothly. Betty might have been happy if she had been able to craft her job to allow for more in-person training. Or found a more fitting job in another company. Research findings show that abandoned goals can create disappointment and poor well-being.[7] Rather than abandoning important goals altogether, reflection and adjustment allows you to transform such goals into objectives that you can accomplish. Special Focus Box 9.3 provides you a brief summary of action tips for the PIERA process.

Special Focus Box 9.3: Self-Managed PIERA Summary

Goal Choice

- Know what you want to accomplish and how you will feel or be different if you accomplish the goal
- Know why you want to accomplish the goal. What is the goal's value to you, your family, your team, your organization?

Planning (Before You Act)

- Figure out HOW you are going to accomplish the goal
- Identify how you will deal with potential obstacles
- Identify the resources you need to help in achieving the goal and to sustain your motivation

Implement and Evaluate

- Get regular feedback and monitor your progress from all perspectives
- Remember to reward your effort and celebrate your successes

Reflect and Adjust

- Debrief – what went right, what went wrong?
- Should I try again? Adjust my goal? Change my strategy?
- What did I learn about my interests? My competencies? My colleagues?

Summary

Leading oneself is a difficult but rewarding skill. As discussed in previous chapters, increasing age diversity in the workforce brings about new challenges in later adulthood. Some of these challenges relate to how to thrive socially in a workplace culture that does not value older employees, other challenges relate to how to adapt one's work role to changing physical abilities and interests. As a leader, the way that you approach these challenges can powerfully influence the attitudes and well-being of your workforce.

We would be remiss if we did not mention a few provisos in your quest to be a better leader for yourself and others. First, a positive attitude is an important resource when attempting to change behavior or relationships. All transitions involve setbacks that can feel at times like utter failure. A positive attitude provides a counter to the sting of failure and smooths the way for evaluating and responding more adaptively to setbacks. When facing setbacks, it is important to recognize *it is normal to feel bad after a failed exchange or poor performance. A positive attitude does not mean that you do not allow yourself to feel bad.* Rather, a positive attitude allows you to acknowledge your emotions but limit the time you dwell on those negative emotions, instead turning your attention toward more productive ways to achieve your goal.

The second concern pertains to self-management during later adulthood. Although research findings suggest that older adults, on average, possess greater skill in emotion regulation than younger adults, the goals that older adults seek to accomplish are often difficult to achieve in the modern workplace. Younger adults tend to hold motives that emphasize extrinsic rewards, such as a promotion or development opportunity. Organizational systems are typically consonant with such rewards, making such rewards a visible incentive for self-managed coaching. In contrast, older adults tend to hold motives that emphasize intrinsic rewards, such as utilizing one's skills, performing meaningful work, feeling valued by younger workers, or job security; outcomes that do not naturally align with organizational reward systems. Nonetheless, we argue that these outcomes can often be achieved within organizations using a proactive, systematic approach such as the one described in this chapter.

Notes

1. Baltes, P. B., & Baltes, M. M. (1990). Psychological perspectives on successful aging: The model of successful optimization with compensation. *Successful Aging: Perspectives from the Behavioral Sciences, 1,* 1–34.
2. Oettingen, G. (2012). Future thought and behavior change. *European Review of Social Psychology, 38,* 69–119.
3. Gollwitzer, P. M., & Sheeran, P. (2006). Implementation intentions and goal achievement: A meta-analysis of effects and processes. *Advances in Experimental Social Psychology, 38,* 69–119.
4. Ashford, S. J. (1986). Feedback-seeking in individual adaptation: A resource perspective. *Academy of Management Journal, 29,* 465–487.
5. Klug, H., & Maier, G. (2015). Linking goal progress and subjective well-being: A meta-analysis. *Journal of Happiness Studies, 16,* 37–65.

6. Fishbah, A., Eyal, T., & Finkelstein, S. R. (2010). How positive and negative feedback motivate goal pursuit. *Social and Personality Psychology Compass, 4,* 517–530.
7. Heckhausen, H., & Kuhl, J. (1985). From wishes to action: The dead ends and short cuts along the way to action. In M. Frese & J. Sabini (Eds.), *Goal directed behavior: The concept of action in psychology* (pp. 134–159). Hillsdale, NJ: Erlbaum.

Index

Printed in the United States
by Baker & Taylor Publisher Services